Wild Turkey Cookbook

WILD TURKEY COOKBOOK

A. D. Livingston

STACKPOLE
BOOKS

Copyright © 1995 by A. D. Livingston

Published by
STACKPOLE BOOKS
5067 Ritter Road
Mechanicsburg, PA 17055

Printed in the United States of America

Cover illustration and design by Mark Olszewski
Interior design by Nick Gregoric

First Edition

10 9 8 7 6 5 4 3 2 1

Other books by A. D. Livingston: *Outdoor Life's Complete Fish & Game Cookbook; Good Vittles; Cast-Iron Cooking; Grilling, Smoking, and Barbecuing; Edible Plants and Animals* (with Dr. Helen N. Livingston); *Venison Cookbook*

Library of Congress Cataloging-in-Publication Data
Livingston, A. D., 1932–
    Wild turkey cookbook / A. D. Livingston. — 1st ed.
      p.   cm.
    Includes index.
    ISBN 0-8117-3097-2
    1. Cookery (Turkeys) 2. Wild turkeys. I. Title.
TX750.5.T87L57   1994
641.6'91—dc20
                                       94-20652
                                         CIP

CONTENTS

	Acknowledgments	vii
	Introduction	ix
ONE	The American Way	1
TWO	Festive Fare	20
THREE	Gourmet Turkey South of the Border	48
FOUR	Grilled and Broiled Turkey	63
FIVE	Skillet Specialties	77
SIX	Stews and Soups	88
SEVEN	Ground Turkey	110
EIGHT	Sandwiches and Loaves	118
NINE	Leftovers and Surprises	124
TEN	Sauces, Dressings, and Go-withs	139
	Appendix A: Ten Steps to Better Wild Turkey	162
	Appendix B: Metric Conversion Tables	169
	Index	171

ACKNOWLEDGMENTS

The author would like to acknowledge recipes quoted or adapted from *Alaska Magazine's Cabin Cookbook* by permission of *Alaska* magazine; *Wildlife Recipes,* by permission of the North Carolina Wildlife Resources Commission; *The South American Cook Book* by permission of Dover Publications, Inc.; *Good Vittles* by permission of Lyons & Burford, Inc.; *A Book of Middle Eastern Food,* by permission of Alfred A. Knopf, Incorporated; *The Smoked-Foods Cookbook* by Lue and Ed Park, by permission of Stackpole Books; and *Food, Fun, and Fable,* by permission of Meme and Charley Publishing Co.

INTRODUCTION

I'm not going to rate the wild turkey on a culinary scale of 1 to 10. Too much depends on the cook and on the individual bird. But I will say without hemming and hawing that the wild turkey in general is better table fare than its domestic cousins. It has more flavor and is more succulent. I have said this a number of times in conversation—and the comment has always drawn a strange look from whoever was listening, as if to see whether I was serious.

I have searched in dozens of books for support to my claim. Somewhat surprisingly to me, many of the fish and game cookbooks don't give much coverage to the wild turkey, usually only two or three recipes. One rather recent fish and game cookbook, published in 1976, makes no mention of this great American game bird whatsoever, although it has several recipes for pigeons.

The best support that I have found comes from an early work by James Beard (published in 1955), in which the master said, "Considered the New World's greatest gift to the gastronomic world, wild turkey has all but disappeared from our tables. We include a recipe for it with the hope that, like the bison, its protection will eventually lead to its availability." Fortunately, both the wild turkey and the buffalo are indeed now available in large numbers. Although the buffalo has to be raised on the range commercially, the comeback of the wild turkey has been nothing short of remarkable.

This book, the first of its kind, offers a number of recipes for cooking wild turkey by several ways, including frying, grilling, and roasting. Tips on dressing and curing the meat are set forth in appendix A, called "Ten Steps to Better Wild Turkey." I won't repeat these steps here, but I will emphasize a cardinal rule: Do not overcook the meat.

In addition to the truly wild turkey, a bird of the wild strain is available from some game or poultry farms. The best of these that I have ever eaten were raised in a large pecan grove, free to roam about and scratch for at least part of their food. In my opinion, these birds make excellent table fare, especially if you can raise your own or get some that are alive so that you will have full control of the butchering process. The really wild birds that are not fed at all are likely to have a little more flavor, but they are not gamy. Of course, birds that have fed heavily on black oak acorns will have a different taste from those that have fed primarily on the sweet acorns of the live oak or on corn or other grain. I personally welcome the variations in flavor—and I cheer for the contrast with the tasteless domestic birds that have been raised in pens or compartments and have never been free to scratch for their daily food. A happy bird makes better eating. Interestingly, a similar feeling seems to be developing about chickens; a few foods experts, including Paul Prudhomme, contend that barnyard chickens have more flavor than supermarket birds. Those of us who remember catching a fryer for Sunday dinner will surely agree.

According to *The Wild Turkey: Biology and Management,* in the mid-1960s fewer than twenty states had spring gobbler seasons. In 1991 every state except Alaska offered a legal spring gobbler season. The wild turkey's numbers increased by more than 1 million between 1985 and 1990. Turkey hunting has increased in popularity, and this trend is expected to continue. Today's hunters have an excellent chance of bagging a turkey during fall or spring hunting seasons, and many states have liberal seasonal bag limits. Parts of Canada and Mexico also offer legal hunting, along with some other countries that have imported and stocked wild birds, such as Australia.

There are several subspecies of wild turkey. The eastern wild turkey inhabits the eastern part of the United States. The Florida wild turkey, sometimes called the Osceola wild turkey, inhabits only the southern part of that state. The Merriam's wild turkey lives in the mountainous areas of the U.S. West. The Rio Grande wild turkey inhabits the southwestern states and northern Mexico. The Gould's wild turkey lives in parts of southern Arizona, New Mexico, and Mexico. A separate species, the ocellated turkey, lives in the lowlands of the Yucatán and adjacent countries in Central America. Some of the above species have also been stocked outside their original range. All of these wild turkeys are excellent eating, making this magnificent bird well worth the hunt.

ONE

The American Way

When I was a strapping boy some years ago, a fishing buddy and I often set out hooks on the local streams for catfish. Looking back, I'm sure that bringing home the meat was a sort of coming-of-age experience for us, and for many other country boys of that era. The channel cat was the prize catch, but we also liked the yellow bullheads, provided they came from running water and were cooked and eaten right away instead of being frozen. We often caught eels along with the cats, but these were greeted with mixed feelings. On the one hand, we were proud of our snakelike catch, but the womenfolks in our families simply didn't care too much for eels, either on the stringer or in the frying pan. I did a little research on the matter and told my buddy that maybe we ought to French cook our eels instead of frying them.

"Shoot," he said. "Anything that can't be fried ain't fit to eat."

Indeed, frying was the American way back then. It still is, really, in spite of calorie counters and cholesterol watchers. For brute flavor and texture, it's hard to beat a piece of crunchy fried chicken or fish. Or turkey. Yet, for some reason, turkey—the great American bird—has never been very popular as frying fare. Why? I can think of at least three reasons.

First, the turkey is a magnificent trophy, and the early hunter, proud about bagging such a bird, wanted to show it off by roasting it whole. This is still the case. Second, the domestic turkey as well as the wild became a festive bird instead of everyday fare, which in turn tended to perpetuate the cook-the-whole-bird mentality. Third, the bird's parts—drumstick, thigh, breast—don't lend themselves ideally to frying simply because they are too large compared with the fryer-size chicken.

1

Yet, the truth is that frying is one of the best ways to cook turkey—both wild and domestic—if you will reduce it to smaller pieces. Fingers cut from a young wild turkey breast are, in my opinion, among the best of all wild game meat. But the meat must be properly cooked and not overcooked. In this regard, most cooks—especially those women who don't hunt—tend to cook all wild game too long simply because it is wild. Chefs often consider any game meat to be strong and somewhat risky to eat. In my opinion, however, the wild turkey, along with most other wild meat, is safer to eat than supermarket fare. At least the hunter can be assured that his meat is fresh and hasn't been given a salmonella bath.

In any case, the recipes below might well change your mind about the best ways to eat a young turkey, wild or otherwise. Naturally, an old tom bird will be too tough when fried, for the same reason that an old barnyard rooster is tougher than a young fryer. As a rule, hen turkeys of all ages are not as tough as old toms, but the younger hens are better for frying. Jakes are my favorites.

There are thousands of recipes for frying chicken, and most of these will work with turkey. Instead of using a thick batter, however, I prefer a simple coating of flour. A thick batter soaks up too much grease to suit me. The recipes below reflect this line of thought, although I do add a recipe or two for batter-fried turkey. (Some people dunk meat into a beaten chicken egg before rolling it in flour or other coating. I don't normally do this simply because the process makes the meat pick up too much flour or other coating. A piece of turkey rolled in flour, dipped in egg, and rolled in flour again picks up a coating that approaches a batter in thickness.)

I normally use all-purpose wheat flour for the coating simply because it is a staple item in my kitchen, but from time to time we have used rye flour, amaranth flour (my wife's favorite), or other flour. Often we mix them with wheat flour.

I have recently heard that chick-pea flour has become very popular in North Africa as a coating for fried foods. In my part of the country, chickpeas are called garbanzo beans. I bought a package in a local supermarket, ground them up into flour, and tried them on fried turkey. It was very good. After trying the chickpea flour, I dusted some turkey strips with *masa harina,* made from cornmeal, and found it to be very good also. In fact, any fine or extrafine cornmeal can be used and was, in fact, the staple of the American Indians and early settlers. In any case, my experimentation has been with light dustings of various flours and breadstuff (such as powdered saltine crackers) instead of with thick batters. If you are a wild-foods enthusiast, as I am, mix in some ground sweet acorns or wild nuts along with a few wild mustard seeds for flavor.

Peanut oil is my choice for frying. It doesn't absorb odors, can be reused several times, and can be heated to a high temperature. Other oils can be used, but most modern practitioners might want to stay away from hog lard and beef suet, although these are very, very good from a strictly culinary point of view.

I usually drain the fried meat on a plain brown bag.

A. D.'s Fried Turkey Fingers

This recipe is one of my favorite ways of cooking breast of wild turkey or pheasant. First, I pull the skin off the breast and cut the meat away from both sides of the breastbone. This leaves two pieces of boneless meat, including the fillet, which is a small piece of very tender meat that grows on either side of the breastbone. (These choice fillets are easily detached from the rest of the breast and can be cooked separately.) Then I cut the meat with the grain into pieces a little larger than the average french fry. It's best to have all the pieces pretty much the same size so that the cooking time will be the same.

> turkey breast meat, cut into fingers
> peanut oil
> all-purpose flour
> salt and pepper to taste

Fillet out each side and cut the meat into fingers as described

3

above. Put $^1/_2$ inch of oil into a skillet. While waiting for the oil to heat, salt and pepper the turkey fingers and dust them with flour. When the grease is quite hot but not smoking, cook the fingers, a handful at a time, turning once, for about 4 minutes or until nicely browned. Do not overcook. Put the cooked fingers on a brown bag to drain, then cook another batch.

When all the turkey is done, pour off most of the grease. Scrape the bottom with a wooden spoon, then add about 2 table-spoons of the flour. Cook and stir constantly until the flour is lightly browned. Slowly add a little water, stirring constantly, until you have a gravy. Serve the turkey fingers with mashed potatoes and gravy, green beans, and the bread of your choice.

Note: This recipe is a good one for cooking in camp. The list of ingredients is short—especially if you plan to bag a wild turkey—and the gravy can do wonders for instant potatoes. My sons like my fried turkey fingers for breakfast, with the gravy atop my wife's wonderful biscuits.

Country-Fried Tom

Here's a recipe to pull out whenever you've got an old tom turkey that would be as tough as jerky if cut into fingers and fried. The secret here is to fillet out the meat on both sides of the breastbone, then cut the meat across the grain into uniform slices $^1/_2$ inch thick. Before cooking, beat the slices with a meat mallet or with the edge of a plate. Beat it soundly, working the plate first one way and then crosswise.

> breast of a large tom turkey
> cooking oil
> flour
> salt and pepper
> cream or half and half

Prepare the turkey breast steaks as described above. After pounding each piece, sprinkle with salt and pepper to taste. Then shake all the pieces in a bag with a little flour. Heat about $^1/_2$ inch of cooking oil in a skillet. On medium high heat, fry the turkey steaks until done, then drain on a brown bag. (Frying too long will make the meat tough or tougher.) When all the pieces have been cooked, pour off most of the oil, saving about 1 tablespoonful. Add about 1 heaping tablespoon of flour and stir constantly until you have a smooth paste. Then, still stirring, pour in a little cream or half and half. Continue cooking and stirring, adding either flour or cream, plus some salt and pepper, until you have a gravy that suits you. Serve the turkey steaks with a little of the gravy over them. Serve the rest of the gravy over rice, mashed potatoes, or biscuits.

If the turkey is still tough after pounding and cooking, all is not lost. Put the cooked pieces into the gravy, add a little water to almost cover the pieces, bring to a light bubble (not a boil), reduce heat, cover tightly, and simmer for half an hour or until the turkey is tender. Add more water from time to time if needed.

Smother-Fried Turkey

If you've got a young turkey, you may want to fry it in recognizable pieces—that is, cut into drumsticks, thighs, back (cut in half), neck, and breast halves. Also include the liver and dressed gizzard if you are so inclined. You can also cut a "pulley bone" piece off the front of the breast.

> 1 young turkey
> cooking oil
> all-purpose flour
> salt and pepper

Cut up the turkey as indicated above. Heat 1 inch of oil in a large skillet. Salt and pepper each piece or turkey, then shake it in a small bag with some flour. When the oil is hot, fill the skillet with the pieces, but don't overcrowd. Unless your skillet is quite large, you'll have to cook the turkey in two or three batches. Cook on medium heat, turning to brown both sides. Drain the browned turkey on absorbent paper. Pour off most of the grease that is left in the skillet. Stir in about 2 tablespoons of flour, then very slowly add a little hot water until you have a thin gravy. Put the turkey pieces back into the skillet, increase the heat until the gravy bubbles, cover tightly, and simmer (but do not boil) for about 30 minutes, or until the turkey is tender. Turn the turkey pieces from time to time, and move them about. Add a little more water if needed. Serve the gravy over mashed potatoes or rice, along with some vegetables and a green salad. A small wild turkey will feed from 4 to 6 people. If you've got a crowd, cook lots of gravy and rice.

Caribbean Fried Turkey

This recipe is cooked in the West Indies with chicken and rum, along with some Oriental soy sauce. I think that the flavors go nicely with breast of wild turkey, as well as with boned thighs. The hot paprika called for in the recipe is sometimes called Spanish paprika. If you don't like hot stuff, then substitute mild Hungarian paprika.

> 1 breast of wild turkey
> 2 cups peanut oil
> flour
> 1/4 cup fresh lime juice
> 1/4 cup golden rum
> 1/4 cup soy sauce
> salt and pepper
> hot or mild paprika

Skin the turkey breast and cut the fillets into chunks about 1 1/2 inches square. In a nonmetallic bowl, mix the lime juice, rum, and soy sauce. Toss the turkey pieces to coat all sides, and marinate at room temperature for 2 or 3 hours. When you are ready to cook, heat the peanut oil in a skillet over high heat. Dry the turkey pieces with paper towel, salt and pepper them to taste, and sprinkle on a little hot paprika or lots of mild paprika. Shake the turkey nuggets in a small bag with about a cup of flour. Reduce the heat to medium and fry a few pieces at a time until nicely brown and done. This will take about 5 minutes, but the time will vary with the temperature of the oil and the thickness of the turkey. Drain the pieces on a brown bag and serve while hot.

Java Turkey

Dubbed the Spice Islands by Marco Polo, Indonesia is indeed made up of thirteen thousand large and small islands that are home to a number of spice plants. Because the islands are far-flung, some of the larger ones have their own cuisine, influenced more or less by the Dutch, English, Indians, Chinese, and Portuguese. The recipe below is from Java, where it is made with yardrun chicken. It is even better when made with breast of wild turkey.

> 1 turkey breast, filleted and cut into fingers
> peanut oil for frying
> 1 cup coconut milk
> 1 medium onion, chopped
> 3 cloves garlic, chopped
> 1 tablespoon red pepper flakes
> 1 teaspoon fresh ginger root, grated
> $1/4$ cup kemiri nuts (or Brazil nuts)
> 2 teaspoons ground coriander
> 2 teaspoons salt
> $1/2$ teaspoon ground turmeric
> 10 strips dried lemon grass (optional)

Zap the onion, garlic, ginger, nuts, red pepper, and coconut milk in a food processor or electric blender until the ingredients are reduced to a smooth paste. (See chapter 10 for information about coconut milk.) Put the turkey fingers (cut about an inch thick) into a pot and add the mixture from the blender. Add the salt, lemon grass, coriander, and turmeric. Turn up the heat, bring to a light boil, reduce heat, and simmer for about 40 minutes, or until the turkey is tender. Stir from time to time so that the bottom won't burn. When the turkey fingers are tender, heat 1 inch of peanut oil in a skillet or wok. Remove the turkey fingers from the pot and fry them for a couple of minutes, or until lightly browned. Do not overcook. Serve with white rice (topped with the gravy left in the boiling pot) and vegetables of your choice. With the last batch I cooked, we served fried eggplant fingers.

Note: Lemon grass is very popular in Southeast Asia and is becoming more widely available in America. It can be omitted from this recipe. Coriander and turmeric are available in most supermarket spice sections. It would be best to use the kemiri nuts (sometimes called candlenuts) native to Indonesia, if you can find them. Any good oily nut can be used, such as Brazil nuts or pecans. Also, if you have your own favorite chili peppers, use them, pulverized, instead of the red pepper flakes.

Easy Turkey Nuggets

These turkey nuggets can be used as an appetizer or as the main meat in a meal. Kids love 'em, partly because they are easy to eat.

> wild turkey breast, cut into 1-inch cubes
> 1 chicken egg, lightly beaten
> ½ cup flour
> ½ cup water
> 1 tablespoon sesame seeds
> salt and pepper to taste
> oil for frying

Mix the egg, water, sesame seeds, and flour. Put a handful of the turkey nuggets into the batter, stir about, and drain. Have ready some hot oil (1 inch deep) in a large skillet. (Or use your deep fryer if you prefer.) Put the batter-coated nuggets into the skillet and fry for 3 minutes. Meanwhile, get another batch ready. After 3 minutes the first batch should be nicely browned. (If not, your oil wasn't hot enough, in which case you should increase the heat and cook until browned.) Repeat the process until all the nuggets have been cooked. I like to use a hand-held strainer to remove the nuggets, then I drain them on a brown bag.

Turkey and Bacon

This recipe, similar to kabobs, is easy to make in a skillet either in camp or at home. In addition to adding flavor, the bacon keeps the turkey from drying out. It's about as foolproof as cooking can be.

> 1 pound wild turkey breast
> thin sliced bacon
> $1/4$ cup peanut oil
> $1/4$ cup soy sauce
> $1/4$ cup sake or vermouth
> 1 tablespoon dark brown sugar
> black pepper (optional)

Mix the soy sauce, sake, brown sugar, and black pepper. Set aside. Cut the turkey breast into kabob-size chunks of about $1^1/_2$ inches. Cut the bacon strips in half. Wrap the bacon around the meat chunks and secure with a round wooden toothpick. Heat the oil in a large skillet, then sauté the turkey chunks until the bacon is nicely browned on all sides. Pour off the oil. Mix in the soy sauce mixture, increase heat until the liquid boils, then decrease the heat and simmer for 5 minutes, turning the turkey chunks once. Serve hot as a side dish or appetizer, or as the main meat course for a meal.

Vietnamese Stir-Fry

The Vietnamese brew a rather strong fish sauce, which they use in cooking rather like the Worcestershire sauce of the West. In fact, Worcestershire sauce itself has fish in it, usually anchovies, but it is not as potent as the Vietnamese stuff. Essentially, the Vietnamese pack small fish in wooden barrels with lots of salt. The liquid that runs off is fish sauce. In spite of the simple procedure, some sauce is better than others, and the Thai sauce, *nam bla*, is a little different from the Vietnamese *nuoc mam*. Either kind can be used in the recipe below, and both kinds are bottled and sold in ethnic markets and by mail order.

The recipe below is designed to feed 2 to 4 people. It can be cooked in a 10-inch skillet or in a wok. If you have a 13-inch skillet or a large wok, you can double the measures. Allow from $1/4$ to $1/2$ pound of turkey per person.

> $1/2$ to 1 pound wild turkey breast
> $1/2$ large pineapple
> 1 rib celery with green tops
> 3 tablespoons peanut oil
> 2 tablespoons fish sauce
> 1 tablespoon cornstarch
> water
> black pepper

Cut the turkey breast into $3/4$-inch cubes, the celery into 1-inch pieces, and the pineapple into $3/4$-inch chunks. Mix 1 tablespoon of cornstarch into 3 tablespoons of water. Heat the peanut oil in the wok or the skillet. The oil should be quite hot, almost to the smoking point. Quickly put in the turkey pieces and 1 tablespoon of the fish sauce. Stir on high heat with a wooden spoon for 2 minutes. Add celery, the pineapple, and another tablespoon of fish sauce. Stir on high heat for 3 minutes. Stir in the cornstarch mixture, and stir for 1 minute. Take the wok or skillet off the heat. Grind a little black pepper over the food and toss lightly. Transfer to a serving platter if you have snooty guests, or serve directly from the wok or skillet for ordinary folks. Serve with fluffy rice.

Tasty variation: The last time I cooked this recipe, we were out of peanut oil, so I fried 4 strips of thick-sliced bacon, cooked the stir-fry in the bacon drippings, and sprinkled the crumbled bacon back onto the dish at the last minute.

Wild Turkey Croquettes

I make this recipe with what's left of the bird after I fillet out the breast. First, disjoint the wings, legs, and thighs, then boil the whole works (including the backbone) in a large pot with a little water.

When the meat is tender, pull it off the bones and weigh out 2 pounds for the recipe below. (Use the rest for sandwiches or salad, and save the stock.) The recipe can also be made with leftover roast turkey, but freshly boiled or steamed meat is better.

> 2 pounds of cooked turkey meat, boneless
> 1½ cups turkey stock
> dry bread crumbs (at least 2½ cups)
> ½ cup flour
> ⅓ cup melted butter
> cooking oil for frying
> 1 medium onion, minced
> 1 hot pepper, seeded and minced
> 2 chicken eggs, beaten
> 2 more chicken eggs, beaten
> salt and pepper

Cool the turkey meat and run it through a meat grinder or zap it in a food processor, or perhaps mince it with a chef's knife. (But don't make mush of it.) Heat the butter in a large skillet and stir in the flour. Add the stock, along with some salt and pepper to taste, and heat until you have a thick sauce. Remove the skillet from the heat and cool a little. Mix in the turkey meat, minced onion, and hot pepper. Whisk two eggs and stir them into the mixture, along with 1 cup dry bread crumbs. Heat some oil for frying in either a skillet or a deep fryer. Beat two chicken eggs in a bowl and pour about 1½ cups of bread crumbs into another bowl. Shape the turkey mixture into oval croquettes. Roll each croquette in the bread crumbs, then dip it into the egg and roll again in the bread crumbs, coating well.

Fry for 2 or 3 minutes on each side if you are using a skillet, or for about 5 minutes if you are using a deep fryer. Drain on brown bags and serve hot.

The measures above will make a rather large batch, enough to feed 6 or 8 people. If you don't need that much, reduce the measures, or better, wrap the cooked croquettes with foil and freeze them for later use. I heat them in the microwave.

Easy variations: Try serving these coquettes with various table sauces, such as Vietnamese fish sauce, Chinese oyster sauce, or Caribbean Pickapepper sauce. Or ordinary ketchup.

Golden Turkey

This recipe makes a beautiful dish when cooked with turkey breast. Although the whole breast can be used, I recommend that you first bone the breast, remove the choice fillets (next to the backbone) for grilling, and cook the other two pieces whole using the recipe below.

> turkey breast halves
> peanut oil
> 3 cups turkey or chicken stock (see below)
> 1 1/2 cups soy sauce
> 3/4 cup sake
> 4 slices fresh ginger root (1/8 inch thick)
> freshly ground black pepper

Skin the turkey pieces. In a boiler of suitable size, mix the turkey stock, soy sauce, sake, ginger, and pepper. The turkey stock used here can be homemade from the recipe in chapter 10, or you can use canned chicken broth. Bring the sauce to a boil and simmer for a while to absorb the flavor from the ginger root. Put in the turkey pieces, bring to a new boil, reduce heat, and simmer for about 30 minutes, or until the turkey is tender. While the turkey simmers, rig for deep frying at 375 degrees. Remove the breast pieces from the sauce and dry them quickly with paper towels. Immediately put the pieces into the hot oil and fry for 4 or 5 minutes, until the pieces are golden. Do not overcook. This recipe works best in a large deep fryer with at least a quart of oil. It can also be cooked in a skillet, but you should fry the pieces of turkey separately.

Note: The stock used for simmering the turkey can be refrigerated and reused several times. Try it for cooking golden fried pheasant.

Wild Turkey Egg Rolls

I have made egg roll skins from scratch, but these days it is much easier to buy them at the supermarket. These are usually available in 1-pound packages, which contain 16 or 18 skins. Thus, for the recipe below you will need 2 packages. The measures can be cut in half if you want to make up only a few, or doubled if you want more. My thinking is that if you are going to rig for deep frying, you might as well cook a batch, then freeze some for later use. The microwave is ideal for thawing out one or two, or more, as needed. They come in handy for a quick lunch, and my boys like them after school as well as during the middle of the night.

I normally use peanut oil, because it can be heated to a high temperature without smoking. Cooking at a high temperature seals the outsides of the egg rolls and keeps them from becoming too greasy. I recommend at least 350 degrees, which is hot enough to seal the juices in and the oil out. Many deep fryers have some sort of basket that fits into them, and these should be heated in the oil before using. Also remember that cooking too many egg rolls at one time will lower the temperature.

For the meat, I prefer turkey breasts that have been poached or steamed until tender. Then I cut the meat with the grain into thin strips or strings.

> 1½ pounds boneless breast meat
> 1 pound bacon
> 2 medium onions, chopped
> 2 stalks celery (with green tops)
> 2 cups bok choy
> about 1 cup chopped water chestnuts
> 1 red bell pepper
> 1 green bell pepper
> 3 chicken eggs
> 2 tablespoons soy sauce
> 1 tablespoon chopped cilantro
> 1 teaspoon grated ginger
> about 3 dozen egg roll skins

Steam, poach, or sauté the turkey and cut with the grain into strings. Fry the bacon in a skillet until it is crisp, then drain and crumble it. Rig the deep fryer and start heating the oil.

Grate the ginger and mix it with the soy sauce in a large bowl. Cut the peppers, celery, and bok choy into strings and mix them in the bowl, along with the chopped cilantro, onion, and water chestnuts. Lightly beat the eggs and stir them in. Add the turkey strings and mix everything well. Put about 1 tablespoon of the mixture on each egg roll skin, stringing out the turkey and vegetables. Fold the egg roll skins over (following the directions on the package), roll, and seal lightly with a little water. Deep fry at 350 degrees until the rolls are slightly browned. Drain. Serve with honey mustard sauce (recipe in chapter 10).

These egg rolls are best when eaten hot, but if you want to freeze some, let them cool and roll each one in plastic wrap. Freeze them a few at the time. To thaw and heat, punch a hole in the plastic wrap and put into a microwave oven for about 1^1/$_2$ minutes.

Remember that the vegetables used in the recipe above are merely recommendations. Try others, such as asparagus or, if you are a wild-foods enthusiast, fresh cattail shoots. In the last batch I made, I used wild Jerusalem artichokes instead of water chestnuts.

Easy Marinated Turkey

I normally cook this recipe with chunks of turkey, preferably from the breast, about 1^1/$_2$ inches thick.

> turkey meat in chunks
> Italian dressing
> crushed garlic
> all-purpose flour
> peanut oil
> salt
> pepper

Put the turkey chunks into a nonmetallic container and pour some Italian dressing over them. Mix in some crushed garlic and black pepper, then toss the meat to coat all sides. Marinate overnight in the refrigerator. When you are ready to cook, heat some oil in a skillet or deep fryer. Drain the turkey pieces and shake in a bag with some flour to which salt has been added. Fry a few pieces at a time over medium high heat until they are golden brown and crispy on both sides. Drain on a brown bag. Repeat until the whole batch has been cooked.

Variation: You can fry larger pieces of turkey using the same recipe, or you can fry smaller pieces to be used as an appetizer. Just make sure that the larger pieces are cooked through, or that the smaller pieces are not cooked to death. Also, you can try other salad dressings for a marinade, but I would suggest that you stick with the clear oil-and-vinegar-based dressings instead of the creamed kind.

Batter-Fried Turkey

This recipe works best in a deep fryer, but it can be cooked in a rather deep skillet with quite a bit of oil in it. As stated earlier in this chapter, a batter is good and crunchy, but it soaks up more grease than a simple coating of flour. The recipe can be made with either chunks or strips of meat, but I do suggest that the turkey pieces be boned before frying. Also, the pieces should be of uniform thickness so that the cooking times will be approximately the same.

> turkey chunks or strips
> 1 cup flour
> 1 cup whole milk
> 1 chicken egg, beaten
> 1 teaspoon baking powder
> $\frac{1}{4}$ cup peanut oil
> additional peanut oil for deep frying
> salt and pepper

Rig for deep frying. If you've got a thermostat on your fryer, set it for 375 degrees. Sprinkle the turkey pieces with salt and pepper. Beat the egg until it is fluffy, then whisk in 1 cup milk and ¼ cup peanut oil. Stir in the flour and baking powder. Dip the turkey pieces into the batter, coating on all sides, and put them into the deep fryer. I dip one piece at a time and put it directly into the deep fryer, then I quickly do another. Do not overcrowd. If you have small pieces, less than an inch thick, cook on high heat until crisp and brown. If you have larger pieces, lower the temperature setting to 300 degrees and cook until crisp and brown. Drain on a brown bag and serve hot.

Buttermilk Turkey with Gravy

This old recipe works best with lard, but modern practitioners might prefer to use a good vegetable oil. The breast of a small turkey, cut into serving-size pieces, is ideal. You can also use the thigh and drumsticks, but it's best to bone these before frying.

> turkey pieces
> buttermilk
> plain milk and water
> flour
> 1 small onion, chopped
> salt and pepper
> cooking oil

Marinate the turkey pieces in buttermilk for an hour or two. When you are ready to cook, heat some cooking oil in a large skillet. Put 1 cup of flour into a bag and mix in 2 teaspoons of salt and ½ teaspoon black pepper. Drain the turkey pieces and shake them, a few at a time, in the flour bag. Fry the turkey pieces a few at a time until they are nicely browned on both sides. Put the pieces on a brown bag to drain. When you have finished frying, pour most of the oil out of the skillet, leaving about 2 table-spoons and the pan drippings. In the remaining oil, sauté the chopped onion on medium high heat for 4 or 5 minutes. Stir in about 2 tablespoons of flour, sprinkling on a little at a time as you stir. Slightly brown the flour, as when making a roux. Slowly pour in a little milk and water, heating and stirring constantly, until you have a gravy of the desired consistency. More flour can be added if needed. Add salt and pepper to taste. Serve the gravy over biscuits, mashed potatoes, or rice, or over the fried turkey pieces, in which case I like to use some minced garlic along with the onion, or better, fresh wild onions with part of their green tops. A wild turkey cooked in camp by this recipe, using bacon drippings and wild onions, is about as good as camp cooking can get.

Oven-Fried Turkey Nuggets

I admit that I have never been a fan of oven-fried foods, although I have eaten some tasty chicken cooked with Shake and Bake and with various recipes. If you've got a favorite recipe for oven-fried chicken, don't hesitate to try it with turkey. Just remember that if you cook large pieces of turkey, the cooking times will be longer.

The recipe below is one of my favorites if the turkey is tender. (Tough birds do better if the meat is steamed or simmered in water for a long cooking time.)

> 2 pounds turkey meat, cut into 1-inch chunks
> $1/2$ cup butter (divided)
> $1/3$ cup grated Parmesan cheese
> $1/3$ cup Italian bread crumbs
> 1 tablespoon Worcestershire sauce

Preheat the oven to 450 degrees. Cut up about 2 pounds of turkey nuggets. I usually get these by skinning and filleting the breast, but the thighs can also be used. Melt half the butter in a pan, and mix in the Worcestershire sauce. Add the turkey nuggets and stir about thoroughly. Mix the bread crumbs and cheese in a brown bag, and shake the turkey nuggets a few at a time to coat all sides. Grease a shallow baking pan, about 10 by 15 inches, and place the nuggets in a single layer. Melt the remaining butter and drizzle on top. Put the pan in the center of the preheated oven, and bake for about 20 minutes, or until the nuggets are nicely browned.

The measures in this recipe can be cut in half if you wish to use a smaller baking pan; reduce the cooking time by a few minutes. Allow at least ¼ pound of meat per adult. I can eat ½ pound if I've got a good bird.

Sessions Whole-Fried Turkey

Frying a whole turkey is not usually very practical, but it can be done with excellent results. I say it's not practical simply because the method requires about 4 gallons or more of cooking oil and a large pot. On the other hand, some cooking oils (I recommend peanut oil) can be used over and over and have a very long shelf life; also, more and more patio cookers are becoming available for frying fish, boiling shrimp, and so on. Some of these are heavy enough to hold a large pot and several gallons of oil. If you ever have occasion to cook several turkeys for a large game supper or some such event, frying may well be the way to go. Once you get rigged up and heat the oil hot, you can fry any number of birds one at a time without the expense of buying more oil.

I got the recipe below from Sessions peanut oil company. It was intended for domestic turkey, but the technique is the same with wild turkey. It is important that you have lots of oil so that when you add the turkey, the temperature won't drop too low. It is also important that the bird be completely covered with oil. Obviously, the first step should be to determine whether you have a large-enough pot and a means of heating it. (The oil should reach 375 degrees, and some small burners simply won't provide enough heat.) Before starting to cook, it's best to test the size of your pot by adding 4 gallons of cold water and immersing the turkey in it, just to make sure that it will fit and won't cause the oil to overflow. Remember that hot oil is very dangerous. Make sure your cooking rig is steady. Plan a way to get the turkey into and out of the pot safely. Sessions recommends tying a cord through the turkey by which to lower and lift it. In any case, be very careful not to drop the bird into the hot oil. A splash can cause burns and create a fire hazard.

> 1 wild turkey, plucked
> about 4 gallons of peanut oil
> paprika
> salt and pepper

Heat the oil to 375 degrees. Sprinkle the bird inside and out with salt, pepper, and paprika. Tie the wings and legs of the turkey with cotton cord. Also tie the cord through the turkey if you plan to lower and raise the bird by this method. When you lower the bird into the pot, make sure that it doesn't become wedged. Fry it for 3 or 4 minutes per pound, moving it about from time to time. The bird is done when it floats to the top. If you don't overcook the turkey, it will be golden brown and succulent.

Note: I don't recommend that you stuff a bird that you plan to fry. Leaving the body cavity open helps it cook through.

TWO

Festive Fare

The turkey was a festive bird long before the Pilgrims celebrated the first Thanksgiving. The fact is that the colonists already knew about the turkey when they landed at Plymouth Rock. The Spanish had discovered the big bird in Latin America, where it had been domesticated centuries earlier, and they took some breeding stock to Europe. The great American bird was so impressive that it quickly replaced the peacock at some banquet extravaganzas and was, like the peacock, served up with all its feathers intact. To accomplish this, the skilled chefs skinned the bird, cooked it, and carefully replaced the skin with every feather in place. Thus, the whole turkey was placed on the table in all its color and splendor.

As the turkey became more widely available in Europe, the Middle East, and North Africa, it tended to replace the domestic goose in rural households. In our own country, it gradually became important mostly as a festive bird, and it remains so today. Most American families simply don't eat turkey except at Thanksgiving or Christmas. This unfortunate situation has really hindered the development of turkey cookery, but people's eating habits are hard to change. Further, most people have eaten turkey cooked in only one way: roasted. This too is unfortunate. Although properly roasted turkey can be very good, most of the turkey consumed in this country is cooked far too long, making it dry and tasteless. Of course, I don't mean to belittle the festive qualities of the whole turkey or the culinary qualities of properly roasted turkey, but I would like to suggest other ways of cooking the bird. Now that the wild turkey is quite plentiful in many parts of the country, and some states have liberal bag limits, perhaps many hunters and their families will want to learn about other ways to cook the meat. After all, the spring gobbler season opens long after the big holiday feasts are done with.

The recipes below set forth several conventional and a few rather unconventional ways to cook a whole bird. I have divided the material into categories, such as Roasted Turkey, Smoked Wild Turkey, Stewing Whole Birds, and Pit Turkey. Before getting into these topics, however, I want to discuss a very important consideration for cooking a whole turkey, or any large chunk of meat: temperature.

The Crucial Temperature: When I first struggled with the material in this chapter, the nation's press and television started doing articles and broadcasts about supermarkets and meat outlets being stocked with contaminated turkey. A report from CBS said that about 95 percent of the U.S. turkey supply was contaminated with salmonella and other bacteria before it hit the market. The way to safe eating, the reports said, was to make sure that the meat was cooked to 180 or 185 degrees. Of course, the normal reaction to such a scare is to make damn sure the turkey is done. This in turn can ruin good meat, making it dry and tough.

Personally, I decided some time ago that a wild turkey is safer for me than market poultry. Why? I have more control over the bird that I bag and field-dress. At least I know it hasn't been run through a salmonella bath at the processing plant. For a while I toyed with the notion of trying to get some data or at least official opinions on whether the wild turkey is indeed safer than its unfortunate slaughterhouse cousins, but I dismissed the idea. Who would give me an unbiased opinion? The Department of Agriculture? The Food and Drug Administration? Who among the bureaucrats could bear being quoted as saying that uninspected wild turkey is safer than inspected and duly stamped supermarket fare?

Although I might appear to be a bit cynical here, the truth is that this "well-done business" was a great setback for me and, I think, for this book and for turkey cookery in general. Whether or not such precautions are necessary from a health viewpoint, I think that a bird cooked to an internal temperature of 185 degrees is too done to be at its culinary best. I thought I had detected a trend in the cooking trade to reduce the temperature somewhat. I've got one fairly new cookbook (published in 1990) that says to cook white turkey meat to 160 or 165 degrees, dark to 175 degrees. I love the 160-degree figure—but is it safe? Frankly, I don't know, and I don't believe anybody else does either. I've seen other temperatures listed in other publications. One book, published in 1984, lists the "takeout" internal temperature to be 143 degrees for the breast, with a "setting time" of 30 minutes. The same book says that a smoked turkey breast is done when the internal temperature reaches 138 degrees—but no-salt fanatics should be warned loudly that the recipe calls for a well-salted turkey breast. So there you have it.

I personally believe that a properly handled wild turkey cooked to 160 degrees and then allowed to coast for a while in the oven before eating will be perfectly safe. In other words, the 160-degree figure might well be safe if it is held for a suitable length of time. But I can't guarantee it. How could I under the circumstances? I do, however, feel comfortable going with the 180-degree figure—and not a hair over—and then yanking the bird out of the oven as soon as that temperature is reached.

I might add that a turkey booklet published by the U.S. Department of Agriculture further complicated this issue by pointing out that white meat is done at 170 degrees, and dark at 180 degrees. So if you are roasting only the breast, you may want to use the 170-degree figure, even though the breast meat of a wild bird runs a little darker than that of a domestic bird.

A good, accurate meat thermometer is essential from both culinary and safety viewpoints. I feel this so strongly that I want to call attention to this instrument under its own heading.

The Meat Thermometer: If you don't have a meat thermometer, read the text above and then buy the best one you can find. It will be your best friend whenever you roast a whole turkey, a venison ham, or any other large chunk of meat. Make sure you purchase one that can be left in the meat during the cooking process. Of these, one type reads like an old-fashioned thermometer with a mercury column scale, and another type has a dial on the end. The dial is much easier and quicker to read. Both types can become covered somewhat with smoke or grease during the cooking process, so that the old mercury column type is especially difficult to read. Other types of meat thermometers work electronically, and newfangled designs are sure to be forthcoming. In any case, remember that it's best to use one that stays inside the meat instead of one that takes instantaneous readings. In other words, it's best to insert the thermometer and leave it there instead of making several holes during the process. Holes let the good juices escape, and this can be very important with a rather dry meat like turkey.

Some people recommend that the thermometer be placed in the thickest part of the inner thigh. My tests with this method have been satisfactory, but with wild turkey I prefer to insert the thermometer into the thickest part of the breast. I insert it from the front and work the pointed tip toward the center, being careful not to touch the breastbone. A guide hole produced with an ice pick makes insertion easier.

Trussing: A whole turkey is easier to handle and cooks a little better if you tie in the wings and legs with cotton twine. With the turkey on its back, pull the legs slightly together, and tie them together by wrapping twine around them just above the knee joints. Snug up the twine and tie off with a square knot. Snug the wings up to the breast and put a piece of twine all the way around the bird. Some people recommend that the wings be turned back behind the back of the bird and tied together.

If the bird is to be stuffed, do so before trussing. Stuffing is covered under the Stuffed Turkey heading.

ROASTED TURKEY

It has become more or less standard in this country to call baked fowl roasted. I suppose it sounds better that way, although I could point out that the term roasted could also apply to cooking on a spit over direct heat. By whatever name, baking is the standard way in America to cook a turkey, although in recent years the patio smoker-cookers have become increasingly popular. Typically, the bird is put into a preheated oven and is cooked at a more or less constant temperature for a certain length of time. The temperature will vary according to the recipe, and the time will vary according to the size of the bird.

As made clear in the preceding discussions, I am a staunch defender of the meat thermometer for baking a whole bird. A few years back, I was recommending that the oven be preheated to only 200 or 220 degrees and held at that temperature during a long cooking period. But this may not be safe. According to USDA Bulletin 243, "This method is *not* recommended. Because of the low temperature, the turkey (and stuffing) might take more than 4 hours to reach a high enough temperature to destroy bacteria, and could be unsafe." The USDA recommends 325 degrees, so I am shifting my position somewhat on this matter. Some of the recipes later in this chapter call for slightly different cooking temperatures, so the oven temperature isn't exact. I might also point out that the thermostat on many ovens isn't accurate anyhow. In any case, as long as you use a meat thermometer, the oven temperature can vary considerably. If it's too hot, however, you'll dry the outer meat before the inside gets done.

Some expert cooks can tell a lot about a cooking turkey just by poking it with their finger and moving the leg joints. When done, the leg moves easily in the joint. I have never trusted this method, especially with wild turkey, but knowing the rule does come in handy from time to time. This feeling, however, is somewhat subjective; that is, the leg might seem to move easily to me (since I don't want the bird well done) and might move rather stiffly to another cook (who might want to make damn certain it is well done).

As a rule, a large oven cooks better and more evenly than a small one. The newer forced-air convection ovens are faster than ordinary at the same temperature and cook more evenly. For vertical roasting, I like the new stands that hold a turkey upright.

Note that some of the outdoor cookers can be used for roasting turkey. These are covered in more detail under Smoked Wild Turkey, but some of the units can be used without the smoke. The silo-shaped water-smokers can be used as an oven simply by leaving out the water and the wood chips. The top-loading units are easy to use, and I like to put a turkey on a vertical stand on the bottom rack.

If you've got a patio cooker that is large enough to hold a turkey without crowding it and will get hot enough to bake the bird, give careful consideration to using it; if you don't have one, take this opportunity to purchase one. Such a unit permits you to bake a turkey on the patio, thereby freeing up the kitchen oven for making dressing, bread, and so on.

I'm not offering a list of recipes for unstuffed oven baked or roasted turkeys, because the process is so simple. But here's what I consider to be the basics:

Easy Baked Wild Turkey

Pluck the bird instead of skinning it. Rub it inside and out with bacon drippings, and sprinkle it with salt. Tie in the wings and feet with cotton twine. Let it sit while you preheat the oven to 350 degrees. Put the bird on a roasting pan breast side up. Insert the meat thermometer and put the roasting pan into the oven. Bake until the meat thermometer reaches 180 degrees. Remove the bird from the oven immediately.

There are any number of variations on this simple process, and some people like to cover a domestic turkey's breast with aluminum foil for at least part of the cooking time. Aluminum foil isn't needed with wild turkey, because the breast is not so thick, but you can use the foil if you wish, with no ill effects. Just fit it around the meat thermometer so that you can read the temperature.

In a common variation, I like to drape strips of bacon across the breast during the baking process. Some people also douse several thicknesses of cheesecloth with bacon drippings and place it across the breast. One of the best turkey breasts I've ever eaten was completely encased in the skin of a smoked ham. Called barding, all such practices are intended to prevent the meat from drying out. Barding is especially recommended with turkey that has been skinned. A similar practice, called larding, requires threading strips of bacon or salt pork inside the turkey breast;

for this purpose special needles are used, but larding needles are hard to find these days. Some people even use a meat syringe to pump oil or fat inside the turkey. I prefer to use strips of smoked bacon atop the bird, but suit yourself.

Most people serve baked whole turkey with a dressing and giblet gravy, both of which are discussed in chapter 10. Some modern cooks hold out for old-timey stuffed turkey, which changes the ball game and requires a new heading.

STUFFED TURKEY

When dressing a turkey or any other bird for stuffing, it is important to leave the skin on the bird; this includes the skin that covers what is known as the crop, so that the bird can be stuffed from both ends. (See appendix A for notes on dressing a bird.) Remember to fill the bird's cavity and crop loosely so that the stuffing has room to expand. The openings often can be closed with skewers, but sometimes it is necessary to use string along with two rows of skewers. The legs and wings also can be tied as usual.

Although I like a stuffed bird very much, I have to tell you that the stuffing itself can be dangerous to your health. Never mix the stuffing until you are ready to use it; this is especially true of any mixture that has raw eggs or oysters in it. To be perfectly safe, make sure that the stuffing is cooked to an internal temperature of 160 degrees. (That figure came from the Department of Agriculture.) If the breast reaches 180 degrees, the stuffing usually will be safe, but not necessarily. A good deal depends on how cold the stuffing was when the bird was put into the oven. If you are using freshly mixed dressing, I don't think it's necessary to insert a thermometer into the stuffing, but it won't hurt a thing to check the temperature after you take the bird out of the oven. Merely remove the thermometer from the breast, run the tip under water to drop the reading down to about 140, then insert it into the center of the stuffing in the cavity. If the stuffing isn't done, quickly remove it from the bird and bake it for a few minutes in a pan.

Some people always remove the stuffing from the turkey before serving it, but I'm guilty of putting the whole works onto the table. I might also add that the modern trend, it seems, is to cook the stuffing in a shallow baking dish and then pile it beside the turkey for serving. In my opinion, this is dressing, not stuffing, although the words are often used interchangeably these days. Most of the stuffing recipes can be cooked separately. Simply put the mixture into a lightly greased, shallow, oven-proof dish and bake it for an hour at 350 degrees. I prefer to cook the dressing inside the turkey, however, because it helps keep the bird from drying out and it absorbs some flavor from the bird. Those who prefer to cook it separately will point out that doing so permits the bird to cook faster and to get done on the inside. This is true. I also concede that dressing, which usually has a lightly browned top, is prettier to look at.

The recipes that follow call for stuffing of one sort or another. Note that some of these are not for ordinary baked turkey and require different cooking methods. Other stuffing recipes can be found in chapter 10.

Bon Secour Wild Turkey

I found this recipe in a book called *Food, Fun, and Fable,* published by Meme's restaurant on the Bon Secour River in southern Alabama. The restaurant, being in a fishing village on Mobile Bay, is noted for its seafood and filé gumbo, but the book does contain a few recipes for and advice on cooking wild game, guinea hens, and so on. Although the recipe leaves you guessing about the exact measures of the stuffing ingredients, most cooks won't have a problem in getting the proportions about right.

The recipe also contains some advice that is worth keeping in mind, and the first sentence can save the day if you simply must roast an old tom:

"If the turkey is large and old it is best to parboil it before roasting, but if it is a young hen it is only necessary to pick, draw, and singe it, wash thoroughly, wipe dry inside, and rub well with salt and butter."

For a stuffing, make a large pan of rich egg bread (see the recipe for corn bread in chapter 10) and break it into small pieces.

In a skillet, sauté some finely chopped onions, bell pepper, celery, and parsley. Turn the contents of the skillet and mix in salt, pepper, sage, and thyme. Also add a pint of freshly shucked oysters and the oyster liquor. Mix in the egg bread. If necessary to thin the stuffing, add a little broth or stock. Then stuff and truss the turkey.

"Place breast DOWN in roaster so that the juices will run down and make breast moist and tender, and roast 20 minutes to the pound in a 325 degree oven. For last hour turn right side up and baste frequently with butter and juices from pan.

"If enough dressing is made, more oysters may be added to the leftover dressing and it can be shaped into patties and fried. . . . This dressing can also be used with oysters omitted and toasted pecan meats and chopped hard boiled eggs substituted."

Crusty Baked Wild Turkey

This creation is certain to please the eye as well as the taste buds, and it is one of the best ways to cook a whole wild turkey. Here's all you'll need:

> young tom or a hen
> 1 cup all-purpose flour
> ¾ cup butter
> fresh lemon juice
> bread stuffing (see recipes in chapter 10)
> salt and pepper

Preheat the oven to 500 degrees. Pluck and dress the bird for stuffing, weigh it, wash it, rub well inside and out with lemon juice, and sprinkle lightly with salt and pepper. Insert a meat thermometer into the thick part of the breast or a thigh, being careful not to touch bone. Melt the butter and make a paste with it and the flour. Spread the paste over the outside surfaces of the turkey, leaving the meat thermometer sticking out. Place the bird breast side up on a rack in a roasting pan of suitable size. (The pan will require a lid later, but do not cover at this point.) Put the bird into the hot oven for 30 minutes, or until the flour paste is set. The exact time will depend partly on the size of the bird. Do not brown the paste at this point.

Reduce the heat to 300 degrees and take out the roaster. Stuff the bird with a bread stuffing of your choice. Pour a cup of water into the bottom of the roasting pan, cover the pan, and put the bird back into the oven for 20 minutes per pound (dressed weight). Remove the cover and bake uncovered until the bird is nicely browned. If the meat thermometer does not read 180 degrees, cover the breast with aluminum foil, leaving the thermometer sticking up, and bake until the thermometer does read 180 degrees.

Use the pan drippings in your giblet gravy (recipe in chapter 10).

Steve Juhan's Wild Turkey Roast

I got this recipe some time ago from a game cookery booklet published by the North Carolina Wildlife Resources Commission. The book was a little sparse on directions, but I assume that the ingredients for the stuffing were peeled and chopped up. In any case, be sure the leaves remain on the celery. I have also added the salt and pepper.

> 1 wild turkey
> 1 apple
> 1 orange
> 1 potato
> 2 or 3 stalks celery
> salt and pepper

Preheat the oven to 325 degrees. (Note: Juhan's recipe suggested an oven temperature of 250 degrees.) Dress the bird for stuffing, then sprinkle it inside and out with salt and pepper. Peel and chop the fruits and vegetables into chunks. Stuff and truss the turkey, then put it breast side down in a roasting pan of suitable size. Add 1 inch of water to the bottom of the pan. Cover the turkey loosely with aluminum foil, and put it into the oven. Bake for 3 or 4 hours, depending on the size of the bird. Baste from time to time with pan drippings, Juhan says, and do not overcook. A good meat thermometer inserted properly into the breast or thigh will help ensure that the bird is done but not overcooked. It should read 180 degrees. Toward the end of the cooking period, you might consider taking off the aluminum foil tent so that the bird will brown nicely. If it seems to be browning too much, cover again with foil until the bird is done.

SMOKED WILD TURKEY

For the record, let me say that most of the recipes in books and magazines for smoked turkey are really for smoke-flavored cooked turkey, not for cold-smoked, uncooked turkey. There are several ways of imparting smoke flavor to turkey before or during the cooking process, and a lot depends on how it is cooked and on the kind of equipment the cook is using.

Obviously, I can't cover every smoker-cooker on the market, much less all the homemade rigs in use across the land. On the other hand, there is a lot of common ground regarding some of the types of smokers and a few other topics, which I'll discuss here, then move on to some recipes using smoked turkey meat.

Silo Water-Smokers. These units typically stand about waist-high and have the shape of a silo. Most of them have a fire box in the bottom, a water pan, two racks, and a removable dome-shaped hood. The heat can be from gas, electricity, or charcoal. Wood chips or chunks can be used in conjunction with any of these types of heat. The water pan can be filled with water or other liquid, and it also catches some of the drippings. Since the water pan sits directly over the source of heat, it is more than a drip pan—it generates steam or water vapor that helps keep the bird moist. Some chefs say they use wine or beer in the water pan, but I see no real advantage to this practice with large chunks of meat, and I consider it to be pretty much a waste of good wine or beer. But suit yourself.

Some units are better than others; in general, price is a good indication of quality. Most manufacturers provide directions for using their units, and their booklets set forth cooking times for various kinds of meat. These are not entirely reliable, and, again,

I think the only foolproof method is to use a good meat thermometer, if you can fit it in for easy reading. I noticed that Coleman once made a unit that had a hole in the side to accommodate a long-stemmed thermometer. This is a great idea, if the hole is in the right place, and anyone who uses a silo smoker often might look around for a long-stemmed thermometer and a drill. (A hole can always be closed with a nail head or bolt of suitable size.) On the other hand, it's a little tricky to insert the thermometer through a hole and then into the bird properly.

Smoking a turkey on some of these units can take a long time (especially on the electric rigs). Moreover, the outside temperature as well as the strength of the wind can have a significant influence on the cooking temperature inside the silo. I recommend that you rub the bird all over with salt and let it sit for a spell before smoking. Of course, it is also possible to smoke a bird in one of these units for an hour or so, then increase the heat for quicker cooking. Note carefully that removing the water pan from the unit (or using it dry) will increase the temperature in the silo; keeping lots of water in the pan will lower the temperature, simply because the heat is used up by converting the water to vapor. (Honest. It's called latent heat of vaporization.) Or you can transfer the turkey to your kitchen oven for quicker cooking.

For initial smoking, I would suggest that you put green oak or hickory, or your choice of green wood, over the electrical unit for a dense smoke. Drying the moisture out of the wood will also lower the temperature inside the silo.

Also remember that heat rises. Therefore, the top rack of a silo unit gets hotter than the bottom rack, unless the bottom is close enough to the fire to be affected by radiant heat when no water pan is being used.

As pointed out earlier, these units can also be used for plain roasting without the use of the water pan or smoke.

I'm not offering a recipe specifically for the silo unit, but anyone who uses the larger models extensively may want to look into the possibility of cooking a barded venison ham (draped with strips of bacon) or perhaps a large chunk of pork on the top rack and simultaneously cooking a small wild turkey or a turkey breast on the bottom rack, arranged so that the juices will drip onto the turkey.

Box Grills: Almost any kind of grill with a lid can be used for smoking, but as a rule the larger units are better. Ideally, the bird should be on one side of the grill and the heat on the other. Add some water-soaked wood chips or green wood to the fire, and you're in the smoking business. It's good to have a meat thermometer in the turkey, and it also helps to have a temperature gauge on the grill. Of course, control of the air flow will help keep the temperature regulated. A properly placed vent will help direct the smoke over the bird. Some of the larger units have a small smokestack for this purpose.

Barrel and Tank Grills: These work exactly like the large covered box grills. That is, the fire is on one end and the heat is on the other. Many of these are homemade, and some are very large. I've even seen them made by splitting tanks and mounting them on boat trailers so that they can be towed from one location to another. Most of the large units that I have seen do a swell job.

Round and Kettle Grills: The round grills can be used for smoking if they are large enough to accommodate a turkey. The essential idea is to put the turkey in the center of the circular rack, rig a drip pan underneath, and spread hot coals and wood chips around the drip pan, making the fire doughnut-shaped.

Pyramid System: This unique cooking system does a fine job on vertical baking, and it is usually quicker than a kitchen oven. It is a charcoal grill that has a rectangular attachment for roasting and smoking. It has a drip pan that can produce vapor from water or beer, and a smoke diffuser that helps spread the smoke evenly. These are rather expensive units made in several sizes from stainless steel, and a 15-inch model is required for cooking a whole turkey. The units are very versatile and should be considered by anyone who needs a highly portable charcoal-burning unit. The whole thing—grill and hood—fits into a flat bag for easy storage. The larger unit is great for camp, but it's too heavy for long-distance backpacking.

Stand-up Smokers: These units are similar to the silo smokers, but they are rectangular and are heated electrically.

Essentially, they are nothing more than a small hot plate and a wood chip pan fitted into a sheet metal box with removable racks. Some are accessed from the front, others from the top, and still others, from both the front and top. They usually have a small electrical unit that is designed more for generating smoke than for quick cooking.

In short, they don't get hot enough to cook a turkey, especially when they are used in cold, windy weather. If you use one of these units, it's best to smoke the bird for a couple of hours for flavor, then transfer it to an oven for cooking. I think you should always use a brine cure or a salt rub cure with these units, especially if you are going to cold-smoke your bird for any length of time. The salt prevents the meat from spoiling, and I feel that it also improves the flavor of the meat. The danger here is to use these rigs for an extended length of time at a temperature that is too high for cold smoking and too low for cooking.

Some of the more expensive of these units can be used for both smoking and for cooking, and have thermostats for this purpose.

Jackleg Smokers: The homemade rigs I've seen for cold smoking sausage and fish and other meats include refrigerators, barrels, one barrel stacked atop another and connected with stove pipe, wooden boxes of one sort or another, pasteboard boxes, and walk-in smoke houses. Some of these do a very good job at what they were designed to do. But remember that a rig for cold-smoking fish won't necessarily work for cooking turkey. The best bet is to cold-smoke the turkey for a couple of hours, then transfer it to an oven for cooking. If you cold-smoke for a long time, remember that plenty of salt (or a brine cure) should be used on the bird inside and out.

Regardless of the rig and cooking method, a smoked turkey can be sliced and eaten at the table just like a regular baked bird. It's even better when it is cold, in my opinion, and is ideal for turkey sandwiches. The meat can be used in most of the leftovers recipes listed in chapter 9 and in most of the soup and gumbo recipes in chapter 6. Here are a couple of other recipes that may suit your fancy or the occasion.

Smoked Wild Turkey with Wild Rice

I like this recipe a lot because it combines two of my favorite wild foods. But it's not mine. I adapted it from *The Smoked-Foods Cookbook* by Lue and Ed Park, who say, "We've had this recipe a long time. In the beginning, we made it with chicken and white rice, but we found it much more flavorful when we substituted smoked birds and wild rice. This dish is good with cheese on top." It sure is.

> ²/₃ cup uncooked wild rice
> 2 tablespoons butter or margarine
> 1 cup chopped onion
> ¹/₂ cup chopped celery
> ¹/₂ cup coarsely chopped green bell pepper
> 1 cup sliced fresh mushrooms
> ¹/₂ teaspoon salt
> ¹/₄ teaspoon pepper
> ¹/₂ teaspoon dried summer savory
> ¹/₂ teaspoon dried marjoram
> ¹/₂ cup blanched almonds, chopped
> ¹/₄ cup minced pimento
> 1¹/₂ cup smoked turkey meat, chopped
> 2 cups turkey stock
> 3 tablespoons flour

Cook the rice according to the directions on the package, and set aside. (Also see my comments on wild rice in chapter 10.) Preheat the oven to 350 degrees. In a frying pan, melt the butter and sauté the vegetables. Add the vegetables to the rice, along with the seasonings, herbs, almonds, and pimento. Stir in the turkey.

Stir the flour into 1 cup of cool turkey stock, then mix until smooth. Heat the remaining stock in a saucepan. Stir in the flour mixture slowly, and cook until it is bubbly and slightly thickened. Add to the rice and turkey. Put the mixture into a greased casserole dish, cover, and bake for 30 minutes, or until it is bubbly. Serves 4.

Smoke 'n' Grill Turkey

In my opinion, a little smoke goes a long way with turkey. On the other hand, I like for the smoke to permeate the meat instead of merely being a surface thing. If you agree with what I am saying, try coating a whole turkey with salt and cold-smoking it for a few hours. Then remove it from the smoker, cut the breast into fingers for this recipe, and use what's left to make one of the gumbo dishes in chapter 6.

> fingers from cold-smoked turkey breast
> bacon drippings
> salt

Rig for grilling. Toss the turkey fingers around in a bowl with a little bacon grease and salt. Grill close to the heat, turning once, for several minutes or until done. If in doubt, cut into the thickest part of a finger before serving.

Variation: Grill as above but baste with a barbecue sauce of your choice. Since the turkey has been smoked, avoid commercial sauces with artificial smoke added.

Open-Fire Roasting

It is possible to roast a whole turkey over a campfire by suspending it from a dingle stick or otherwise hanging it above or beside the fire. I would recommend that you leave the feet on the bird, then cross the legs and tie them with wire so that the whole thing can be suspended safely. If you are cooking over a campfire, it's best to devise some means of quickly adjusting the distance between the bird and the fire. Otherwise, your bird might burn on the outside before it gets done on the inside. Or you might consider a means of adjusting the fire. Building a large fire and then raking out some coals for cooking might be the best way to go. The old keyhole fire, in which wood is burned inside rocks placed in the shape of a keyhole, works well. The large end is used for the main fire, and the small end for cooking. Of course, a spit for constantly turning the bird comes in handy if you've got a good one.

A whole bird can also be roasted successfully above large patio grills, and even at a hearth, as shown in the next two recipes.

Missouri Turkey on a Spit

One of the best methods for cooking a whole bird came my way via a book published by the Missouri Department of Conservation, called Cy Littlebee's *Guide to Cooking Fish and Game*. (The recipe was submitted by Jane H. Latham.) In the version below, I have modified the procedure a little, but the ingredients are the same. To cook the bird to perfection, you will have to put it on a spit and turn constantly. Of course, the modern electric rotisseries are ideal, if you've got a good one. I like the bird cooked with charcoal or wood coals, but gas or electric grills rigged with rotisseries will also work.

> 1 wild turkey
> 1 cup sherry
> 1 cup butter
> celery tops or parsley
> 1 tablespoon salt
> 1 teaspoon black pepper
> 1 teaspoon thyme

Rub the turkey inside and out with about half of the sherry. Sprinkle it lightly inside and out with a mixture of salt, pepper, minced parsley, and thyme. (Use only part of the salt mixture, saving the rest for the basting sauce.) Spit the bird according to the manufacturer's instructions for your equipment. Carefully insert a meat thermometer into the thickest part of the bird's thigh, being careful not to touch bone or the spit. Start cooking over a medium hot fire or medium heat. Melt the butter, and stir in the rest of the salt mixture and sherry. Baste often. Cook for several hours, until the meat thermometer reads 180 degrees. (See the discussion of internal temperature and meat thermometers earlier in this chapter.)

Jane Latham said to serve the bird with mashed potatoes

beaten to a froth with butter and cream, corn on the cob, thin-sliced tomatoes, and red or white wine. Who could argue with that?

Colonial Turkey

This recipe was originally published in *American Cookery* way back in 1796, which was the first cookbook to be written and published in the New World.

The grammar is not quite what the reader sees in modern cookbooks, but it's easy enough to figure out. Beef suet is a beef fat used for cooking. Modern readers can substitute margarine or Crisco. A gill of wine is ¼ pint.

"One pound soft wheat bread, 3 ounces beef suet, 3 eggs, a little sweet thyme, sweet marjoram, pepper and salt, and some add a gill of wine; fill the bird therewith and sew up, hang down to a steady solid fire, basting frequently with salt and water, and roast until a stream emits from the breast, put one third of a pound of butter into the gravy; serve up with boiled onions and cranberry-sauce, mangoes, pickles, or celery."

STEWING WHOLE BIRDS

Modern Americans don't often boil or stew turkeys, preferring to stick them into the oven. Our forefathers, on the other hand, often cooked them in an iron pot suspended over a fire in the hearth, and boiling was a very common way with all meats. Remember that the electric or gas oven is a fairly recent invention; with an open hearth, boiling or cooking on a spit was the easiest way to go. Boiling was, and still is, a very good way to cook most meats, including turkey. Here are some recipes to try.

Turkey with Stewed Oysters

This recipe calls for lots of oysters, which were plentiful along the Atlantic coast during Colonial days. Some people can still gather their own oysters, but be warned that this recipe might put a strain on the food budget if you have to buy them.

In any case, this recipe works well for tough old birds as well as for young toms and hens.

> 1 turkey, plucked and dressed whole for stuffing
> 1 gallon of hulled oysters
> salt and pepper to taste
> parsley or celery tops, chopped
> butter
> water

Stuff the turkey with oysters that have been patted dry with paper towels and sew the opening shut. (Reserve a pint of oysters for stewing.) Put the turkey into a pot of suitable size, and add enough water to barely cover it. Bring to a boil, reduce heat, and simmer until the bird is tender. (An old bird will take two hours or longer.)

Meanwhile, stew the rest of the oysters in a suitable pan with a little water, salt, pepper, chopped parsley, and butter. When the turkey is tender, place it on a large platter and pour the stewed oysters over it.

Serve with vegetables, cranberry sauce, and hot bread. Also try raw Jerusalem artichokes with this dish, if you've got them on hand or can dig some along a fencerow.

Middle Eastern Stuffed Turkey

The Middle East might seem to be a strange source for one of my favorite recipes for cooking a whole American wild turkey. Yet, consider the following words from Claudia Roden's *A Book of Middle Eastern Food*: "In the Middle East, turkeys range very freely and are small and tough, more like game birds. So they are usually stewed rather than roasted. This makes the flesh very juicy, and helps it to absorb the flavors of the stuffings as well as the seasonings in the stock. A very large pan is required to hold the bird."

Note carefully the words about the large pan, and remember that it must be able to hold the bird in enough water to cover it. Large stock pots are available, and, of course, you can also use the old black iron wash pots. In any case, here's the recipe, which is very close to Ms. Roden's.

> 1 wild turkey
> 2 pounds ground beef or lamb
> 2 cups chopped nuts, such as pistachios or pine nuts
> 2¹/₄ cups long-grain rice
> ¹/₂ cup raisins
> lemon juice
> oil or butter
> salt and black pepper
> 1 teaspoon ground cinnamon
> ¹/₄ teaspoon ground allspice
> water

Pluck the bird, wash it, and rub it inside and out with freshly squeezed lemon juice. Set aside. In a saucepan or skillet, heat 2¹/₂ tablespoons butter or oil and brown the ground meat. Add the nuts and stir-fry for 3 minutes. Then add the rice and stir-fry for another minute or two. Add the raisins, salt, pepper, cinnamon, and allspice. Mix well. Stuff the turkey loosely so that the rice will have room to expand.

Heat 6 tablespoons of butter or oil in the large cooking pot or a wide skillet. (A large skillet makes it easier to turn the bird to brown all sides.) When the bird is browned, cover it with water in the pot. Add some salt and pepper. Bring to a boil, reduce heat, and simmer gently for 2 to 3 hours, depending on the size of the bird and how tough it is. Sticking a fork into the meat is usually a pretty good test. Turn off the heat and leave the bird in the liquid while it cools down a little. Then take the bird out and let it drain on a platter. Serve it either whole or cut into pieces piled atop the stuffing. Moisten with some of the stock. You can also use some of the stock to make giblet gravy, if you are so inclined.

This turkey is so moist and good that you may decide it's the only way to cook a whole wild turkey. It makes even domestic turkey succulent.

Soused Tom Turkey

Here's a good stove-top recipe for a tough bird. You'll need a large, oblong roasting pan with a tight-fitting lid, suitable for putting on two stove eyes or burners. You'll also need a rack to hold the bird off the bottom. Try devising a rack with venison ribs, which will add to the flavor of the gravy.

> 1 tom turkey, plucked and drawn
> 3 slices bacon
> 2 medium onions, sliced
> 2 carrots, chopped
> 2 stalks celery, chopped
> 2 cloves garlic, minced
> $\frac{1}{2}$ cup chopped parsley
> 1 tablespoon chopped fresh thyme
> 2 bay leaves
> 2 cups hot water with 2 chicken bouillon cubes added
> $\frac{1}{2}$ bottle dry white wine
> salt and pepper
> flour
> water

Wash the dressed bird, sprinkle inside and out with salt and pepper, and truss with cotton twine. Put the pan over two stove eyes, and insert the rack or build one with bones. (I have also used two iron trivets to form a rack.) Scatter the onions, garlic, carrots, celery, parsley, thyme, and bay leaves over the rack. Pour the bouillon water and wine over the vegetables. Place the turkey on top, breast side up, and drape the bacon over it.

Turn on the heat, bring to a boil, reduce heat, cover tightly, and gently simmer for several hours, or until the turkey is very tender. Add a little water from time to time, if needed. When the bird is quite tender, carefully remove it from the rack and place it on a serving platter. Throw out the bay leaves and the bacon. Make a paste by stirring a little flour into a little water, then slowly add this to the liquid in the pan on low heat, stirring as you go. Stir and heat until you have a smooth gravy. Thin with a little plain water if necessary, and add a little salt and pepper if desired. Serve the gravy in a bowl. I like to pile rice around the edges of the turkey, maybe with a garnish of green stuff and red crab apples, and put the whole works onto the table. Steamed turkey is relatively easy to "carve," and the meat will almost fall off the bone.

Note: If you want to cook a whole bird in camp, this may be the way to go, partly because the method requires no oven. A two-burner camp stove can be used for heat, or you can use coals from a campfire, if you have time to tend such a fire. You can also dig an oblong pit and fill the bottom with hot coals, put in the roasting pan, and cover the whole works up with the dirt that came out of the pit. Then you can go hunting while your bird cooks. Usually, the bird will be done after 8 hours; if not, finish the job on a new campfire or atop a camp stove. The list of ingredients above may be a little long for toting to camp; if so, try plain water, 3 onions cut into quarters, salt, and pepper, along with a few chopped wild onion tops or watercress.

PIT TURKEY

Some of the best meats are cooked in a hole in the ground, and wild turkey can be cooked by this method. Start by digging a hole about 3 or 4 feet deep and 3 feet across. Pile the dirt off to the side, out of the way but still handy. Build a good wood fire on top of the hole, using plenty of wood in long pieces. As the fire burns down, push the end pieces inward into the hole, but also maintain a fire on the side. Let the fire burn down to coals.

Exact cooking times aren't critical, but timing is important. Start a day ahead. Dig the hole in the afternoon and lay the fire. Light the fire at about 11:00 P.M. Tend the fire, hoping that it will burn down just right by midnight.

While waiting for the fire to burn down, get the meat ready. Use a whole turkey, preferably plucked. Wash it thoroughly, then rub it inside and out with freshly squeezed lemon juice. Let this stand a few minutes, then rub it with bacon drippings. Next, sprinkle it liberally inside and out with salt and black pepper. Don't spare the salt. Place the turkey, breast up, on a large piece of extra-heavy aluminum foil. Drape 3 or 4 thinly sliced pieces of bacon over the breast. (Thick slices will make the gravy too greasy.) Tie in the legs and wings with cotton twine. Make sure that no sharp bones stick out to pierce the aluminum foil. Cover the bird with another piece of aluminum foil, then crimp the foil all around. If you've got room, it's best to overlap the edges of each side by at least 1 inch, preferably more. Run the seam between your fingers to seal, then make another fold. The idea is to seal in the steam and, hopefully, the juices.

After sealing the bird, give some thought to how you are going to get it into and out of the pit. This can be dangerous, so have a designated pit man if this is a festive beer-guzzling activity. I usually wrap some wire around each end and form a sort of bail about a foot above the breast. If you try this method, be careful to avoid wire that has any sort of coating on it. You don't want any toxic fumes in the same hole with your meat.

When everything is ready, lower the bird carefully onto the coals (breast side up). Cover the top with coals from the surface fire. Then cover the whole works with dirt, filling the hole all the way to the top. At about 11:00 the next morning, dig out the dirt, being careful not to puncture the aluminum foil. Slowly, carefully, lift the turkey out by the wire and brush the dirt off the foil. Slit the top part of the aluminum foil and transfer the turkey to a platter. The meat should more or less fall off the bone, so you have to proceed carefully once again when you transfer it to a serving platter.

The aluminum foil makes this recipe easy. The accomplished pit cook, however, will no doubt insist on wrapping the turkey in burlap or in leaves of one sort or another. Even cabbage leaves or green corn shucks. I offer no advice in this matter, but I have to add that some of the very best pit-cooked foods make use of the leaves or other covering as a flavoring agent. As the American Indians knew, steaming seaweed added a good flavor and aroma to a New England clam bake. As the ancient Polynesians knew, ti leaves helped flavor the luau. As the Aztecs knew, the leaves of the agave plant helped flavor the barbacoa—and these leaves are still used in Mexico and here and there in the south of Texas.

(The Maya of the Yucatan used banana leaves.) Anyone who has access to fresh agave or banana leaves or ti leaves is encouraged to experiment. Remember that the ancient Mexican dish is cooked on a rack of woven green limbs (the *barbacoa*). This rack is placed over a sort of tray and vegetables are placed over the meat or around it. The juices from the meat, vegetables, and agave leaves collect in the tray. This sauce, amplified with pulque, a beer made from the agave bulb (also the source of tequila), is served over the meat. Further details can be found in Elisabeth Ortiz's *The Complete Book of Mexican Cooking.*

If you don't have agave leaves and pulque, aluminum foil will get you off to a very good start with pit cooking. If you like, wrap grape, collard, or spinach leaves over the turkey, then wrap the whole works in foil. Also try green leaves from corn stalks, or shucks from roasting ears. I have lined the bottom of a piece of heavy-duty aluminum foil with wet corn shucks before putting the turkey down. Of course, I leave a wide margin around the edge of the shuck lining so that the bottom sheet of foil can be sealed to the top sheet.

Be warned that digging a hole of suitable size can be quite a bit of work, especially in hard ground with lots of roots in it. If you are going to this much trouble, you might as well cook a ham of venison or some other large chunk of meat, such as a 10-pound boned leg of lamb or a sirloin tip, along with the turkey. Put the chunk of meat onto a piece of foil and bend up the edges a little. Wipe the meat all over with vinegar, then sprinkle it with salt and pepper. Drape 3 or 4 strips of thin bacon over the meat. Surround with some onions and garlic. Seal according to the directions above.

Be warned that pit cooking is not a foolproof technique. In all honesty, I must refer you to step 6 in appendix A.

COOKING THE BREAST

Most people argue that the breast is the best part of the wild turkey (or any other fowl), but a few hold out for the thighs and legs. A few others might champion the giblets. But most will agree that a whole turkey is a bit much to serve a small family, unless the hunter wants to display the bird. Often, the breast alone will be quite enough, and it is almost always easier to cook and carve than a whole bird. Also, it doesn't take up as much room on the table. Most of the whole-bird recipes that do not call for stuffing can be adapted to a breast-only approach. And remember that most stuffings can be cooked separately and used as dressing.

In any case, you might want to try the following recipes with or without dressing.

Baked Turkey Breast

Here's a good recipe for baked turkey. It can be cooked with a whole breast (bone-in), but I prefer to cut out the two breast fillets and then tie them back together with a little bacon in the middle.

> 1 turkey breast, filleted
> bacon
> 1 large onion, minced
> 1 tablespoon minced fresh parsley
> $1/2$ cup margarine or butter
> juice of 1 lemon
> 1 teaspoon powdered mustard
> $1/2$ cup white wine
> salt and pepper to taste
> paprika

Preheat the oven to 300 degrees. Fillet the breast, leaving the skin on. Sandwich 2 strips of bacon between the breasts, then tie the two halves together with cotton string or stick them together with skewers. (You'll need to secure both ends and the middle.)

Melt the butter in a saucepan or small skillet. Sauté the onion and parsley for 5 minutes. Stir in the lemon juice, mustard, salt, and pepper. Simmer this sauce for 5 minutes.

Grease a small baking dish and put the tied turkey breast in it with the skin side up. Insert a meat thermometer into the thickest part. Pour all the sauce over the top of the breast. Drape several slices of bacon over the breast. Bake in the oven for about 1 hour, basting two or three times with the juices from the pan. After baking for 1 hour, pour the wine over the turkey breast. Then bake until the thermometer reads 170 or 180 degrees (see the comments under "The Crucial Temperature" and "The Meat Thermometer" at the beginning of this chapter), basting every 5 minutes or so with the juices from the pan. When the turkey is almost done, sprinkle it with paprika. Put the turkey breast onto a small platter and carve it at the table. Serve the pan drippings as gravy on the sliced turkey and perhaps on rice.

Rock Salt Roast Turkey Breast

One of my favorite ways for cooking a venison roast can also be used to cook a breast of wild turkey. Because of the high heat used to cook the recipe, it is essential that a meat thermometer be inserted into the thickest part of the breast.

>wild turkey breast
>bacon drippings
>powdered mustard
>black pepper
>lots of rock salt
>1/4 cup brandy

Preheat the oven to 500 degrees. Select a shallow baking or small roasting pan that is suitable for putting onto the table. Rub the turkey breast all over with bacon drippings, then sprinkle it lightly with powdered mustard and black pepper. Fit the turkey into the pan skin side up. Pour rock salt all around the turkey breast. Insert the meat thermometer deep into the breast, but do not touch bone. Build up a mound with rock salt, completely covering the turkey with at least an inch of salt. Wet your hands and moisten the mound a little. Put the pan into the center of the oven. Immediately reduce the heat to 300 degrees. Cook for 10 minutes per pound of meat, then start checking the meat thermometer from time to time. Bake until the thermometer reaches 170 or

180 degrees (see the comments under "The Crucial Temperature" and "The Meat Thermometer" at the beginning of this
chapter). Turn the oven off and let the bird coast for 10 minutes.
Remove the pan and crack off the rock salt by whacking it with a
large spoon or hammer. I do this at the table, because I consider
the show to be part of the recipe. Remove all the salt from the
sides of the breast. Have ready ¼ cup of warmed brandy. (I use a
ladle.) Set the brandy afire and pour it over the turkey breast.
Carve at the table. Serve with vegetables and pickled crab apples
or homemade cranberry sauce. (See recipe in chapter 10.)

Variation: If you've got a larding needle and don't mind a
little hog fat, insert some strips of salt pork inside the breast, or
drape thin strips of bacon over the breast before roasting it.

Roast Breast of Wild Turkey

I like this recipe not only because it is good, but also because the
turkey cooks along with another kind of meat for those who think
they don't like wild turkey.

> 1 breast of young turkey
> 1 pound cured ham (preferably a center-cut slice)
> 8 to 12 ounces fresh mushrooms, whole
> 8 to 12 ounces small white onions (or shallots), whole
> ¼ cup butter
> 1 cup white wine
> salt and pepper (or lemon-pepper seasoning salt)

Preheat the oven to 350 degrees and melt the butter. Brush
the bird with melted butter, then sprinkle lightly with salt and
pepper or with lemon-pepper seasoning salt. Put the breast into
a small roasting pan, preferably oval in shape. Chop the cured
ham into 2-inch chunks. Peel the onions. Arrange ham, onions,
and mushrooms around the turkey breast. Pour the wine over the
meats and vegetables, then sprinkle lightly with salt and pepper.
Cover the dish with aluminum foil. Bake for about 1½ hours.
Remove the aluminum foil, and insert a meat thermometer into

the thickest part of the turkey breast, being careful not to touch bone. Cook until internal temperature reaches 180 degrees. Ideally, the bird will be nicely browned at the same time. If it starts to brown too quickly, cover the bird and vegetables with aluminum foil, leaving the thermometer sticking out for easy reading. Serve hot with vegetables. The pan gravy, which goes nicely with rice or mashed potatoes, can be thickened by slowly stirring in a small amount of paste made with flour (or cornstarch) and water.

Breast on a Rotisserie

If you've got an electric rotisserie that fits over your outdoor or stove-top grill, be sure to try a breast of wild turkey on it. Spit and balance the breast according to the directions for your unit, then insert a meat thermometer into the meat, running it more or less parallel with the spit so that it won't be in the way. Rub the breast with bacon drippings and salt, then baste it from time to time with a good basting sauce. A thick barbecue sauce can also be used, but note that most really thick sauces tend to burn if they are applied too early in the basting process. For long basting, use juice or oil. Freshly squeezed pomegranate juice is popular for basting roast turkey in southern Italy. I recommend it highly, if it is available. Also, a syrup made from pomegranate juice (see recipe in chapter 10) can be used during the last 10 minutes or so of basting. If you don't have pomegranate juice, try lemon juice or the juice of sour oranges. Freshly squeezed onion juice is also good.

THREE

Gourmet Turkey South of the Border

The American wild turkey, in one species or another, once ranged over parts of Canada, most of the United States, and almost all of Mexico. A separate species, the ocellated turkey, inhabited the lowlands of the Yucatán and contiguous parts of Central America. Folk tales of the pre-Aztec Indians indicate that the wild turkey was a sacred bird, and, of course, the feathers were highly prized by many Indian tribes.

The turkey was first domesticated in Mexico or possibly in the southwestern part of the United States. This event was no doubt connected with the development of agriculture, and especially of corn, which would on the one hand attract the turkey closer to Indian villages and on the other hand make it more desirable to control the bird's comings and goings.

Corn gave the Indians more freedom to pursue cultural matters, including the development of a ruling class and a class of professionals other than farmers. The first professional chefs in the New World probably developed in the Aztec area of central Mexico, in the Maya culture in the Yucatán, or, perhaps, in the Inca culture down in the Andes. The world's most famous turkey recipe—*Molé de Poblano de Guajolote*—came from the Aztec camp and called for an unusual ingredient. Unusual, that is, to most modern peoples—but not to the Aztecs. I'm talking about chocolate, an American food. The Aztecs used lost of chocolate and always in its natural bitter form, although for some purposes they mixed in a little vanilla bean. The use of chocolate in recipes for meats has never really caught on in the modern world, but a few recipes for game and game birds still list it as an ingredient. And regional turkey recipes as far north as Texas call for it. I have had my doubts about using chocolate in meat recipes, and I said so in some of my earlier writings, but I have to take it all back. It can be delicious in a properly made molé, along with some other great American ingredients such as chili peppers, peanuts, pine nuts, pumpkin seeds, tomatoes, and squash seeds. Honest.

Molé de Poblano de Guajolote

Like Brunswick stew and chili, this famous recipe has thousands of variations. Many of the recipes tend to have a very long list of ingredients, including, often, several kinds of peppers. In fact, the recipe included here, adapted from *The South American Cook Book*, has no fewer than 25 ingredients. (Don't worry; a shortcut is listed at the end.) Essentially, the dish is merely a disjointed turkey stewed in hot sauce with some bitter chocolate in it. Of course, there are many regional variations, and the peoples of the Yucatán (of Mayan influence) are apt to argue for annatto seeds, which are also used in the Caribbean islands. Also called annatta, achiote, urucu, and roucou, these seeds are used as a flavoring and as a food colorant. In any case, Mexican cuisine is highly developed and has a very long history. I consider the following recipe to be authentic. Although it does show some Spanish or European influence, most of the ingredients, such as squash seeds and peanuts, are native to the Americas. Further, the turkey itself was a major festive bird in Mexico as well as north of the border, and on south to Peru. The following is from *The South American Cook Book*.

"We eat turkey ceremoniously on Thanksgiving, while in Latin America it is the chief food at a number of feasts. In Mexico a fine gobbler decked with wreaths of flowers is often presented by the mother of the bride to the godparents at a wedding, and the importance of a marriage is measured by the number of turkeys killed. Such a feast is called a Molé, as is also the celebrations of the Saint's Day of a district or city ward.

"An American friend tells of going with her engineer husband in the early days to an isolated mining camp in Sonora where they lived comfortably enough in an adobe house furnished by the company. She grew unbearably homesick, and when Christmas came longed for an American celebration with roast turkey, so her husband gave their cook one rifle cartridge and sent him out on the mountain where wild turkeys flocked, explaining that a turkey had become necessary for the happiness of the household. At nightfall the man came back with an enormous bird, standing five feet from the tips of its claws to the bullet-holed head. He was proud of the turkey, but still more proud of his perfect shot.

"The next morning the wife was up early to superintend the stuffing and cooking of the fowl. But the cook was earlier still. He had cleaned the turkey, jointed it, and had it already stewing in a pot. His mistress was in tears, and the dismayed servant was nearly on his knees in despair over having unwittingly cut it up to prepare it in a style his employers considered most un-American.

"It was a sad Christmas morning until the midday meal was served, and the strange dish came on the table. It was *Molé de Poblano Guajolote* [turkey in Mexican people's sauce], often simply called *Molé de Guajolote*, which would elevate the cuisine of any country to the epicurean class. When the family tasted it all their gloom fled, and the cook was the happiest man alive.

"Herewith the recipe, with all 25 ingredients.

> $1/2$ pound pasilla peppers
> $1/2$ pound broad peppers
> $1/4$ pound brown peppers
> 4 to 10 chilies
> 3 cups olive oil or butter
> 1 large turkey, jointed
> 1 tablespoon sesame seeds
> $1/2$ cup squash seeds
> $1/2$ cup pumpkin seeds
> $1/2$ cup peanuts
> 2 tablespoons pine nuts
> 1 piece stale tortilla
> $1/2$ slice white bread
> 3 to 6 garlic cloves, minced

3 tomatoes, chopped
1 sprig marjoram
1 sprig thyme
1 bay leaf
3 cloves
1 teaspoon cinnamon
$1/2$ teaspoon ground ginger
1 tablespoon aniseed
$1/2$ cup raisins
salt
1 ounce unsweetened chocolate

"Remove seeds and veins from peppers and chilies and fry in plenty of oil. If dried peppers are used drop them into hot water to soften and let stand; then drain. Fry turkey in pepper-flavored oil until brown on all sides. Arrange turkey pieces close together, preferably in an earthenware casserole, but a deep saucepan will do. Cover with salted boiling water and cook gently until tender. Toast the sesame seeds by shaking over heat in a dry pan. Fry squash and pumpkin seeds but do not brown. Roast peanuts, if not already roasted. Fry tortilla and bread until crisp, then crumble it. Finely grind sesame, squash, and pumpkin seeds, pine nuts, [peanuts], and bread crumbs. Also grind peppers and chilies together. Slowly fry garlic without browning. Add tomato and fry until tomato thickens. Put all these prepared flavorings together. Mash and work mixture until smooth. Add strained oil from various fryings to herbs, spices, and raisins and mix thoroughly, seasoning to taste with salt. Simmer and stir with wooden spoon. Add turkey and its broth and finish cooking, moving it once in a while with a wooden spoon to prevent sticking. Add grated chocolate at the last moment and take up when melted and blended.

"This long process may be shortened to kitchenette technique by buying a tin of Molé de Guajolote at a Spanish store and using it according to the directions for the preparation of a small turkey, the vest-pocket kind being bred nowadays to fit the family refrigerator."

Larded Turkey

An old Mexican recipe calls for larding a chicken with bacon. I think that larding works even better with turkey breast, which tends to be on the dry side, and I highly recommend it for those among us whose diet will permit the addition of a little fat. You'll need a larding needle, however, which may be hard to come by these days. Essentially, it's a large needle used to insert strips of bacon or salt pork into a piece of meat, and at one time it was widely used in venison cookery.

My variation of this recipe calls for cilantro in the sauce. Sometimes called Chinese parsley or Mexican parsley, this ingredient has become increasingly available in recent years. (If you grow your own cilantro, use the roots as well as the leaves.) Coriander seeds are also from the cilantro plant.

The Bird
1 turkey breast
2 or 3 slices of salt pork
2 cloves garlic, grated
1 teaspoon chili powder
2 allspice berries, crushed
1 tablespoon chopped cilantro
salt and cayenne pepper
flour
bacon fat

Preheat the oven to 500 degrees. Mix the chili powder, salt, cayenne, chopped cilantro, garlic, and crushed allspice. Rub the turkey breast with spices. Cut the salt pork into strips small enough for use with the larding needle. Insert 4 strips of salt pork into each side of the breast, working it in lengthwise and nicely spaced. Coat the turkey breast with bacon grease, then sprinkle it all over with flour. Insert a meat thermometer into the breast, being careful not to touch bone. Grease a roasting pan (just large enough to hold the turkey breast) and fit the turkey breast into it so that the thermometer will be visible. Put the pan into the hot oven for 15 minutes. Then reduce the thermostat to 250 degrees and cook until the thermometer reads 180 degrees. (See the discussion of internal temperature and meat thermometers in chapter 2.)

As soon as the turkey is in the oven, mix the following.

The Basting Sauce
$1/4$ cup melted butter
2 cups tomato juice
1 green pepper, seeded and grated
1 small onion (golf-ball size), grated
2 cloves garlic, grated
1 tablespoon minced cilantro leaves (and roots)
1 teaspoon ground coriander seeds
1 tablespoon peanut butter or crushed peanuts
salt and pepper

Heat the butter in a skillet or saucepan, then stir in the other ingredients and heat through. Pour the mixture over the turkey breast, and baste with it every 20 or 30 minutes. Add a little water to the pan if needed.

When the turkey breast is done, let it cool and set a little, then slice it and arrange the pieces on a serving platter. Pour the sauce from the pan over the meat.

Mexican Stuffed Turkey

The popularity of the molé notwithstanding, the turkey is some-times stuffed in Mexico, a technique that will seem more festive to Americans north of the border. Here's a good recipe that combines roast turkey with several genuine Mexican ingredients—including bitter chocolate. The problem with most of the good Mexican recipes I have found is that they call for ingredients I can't pick up at the local stores. I have one that calls for 8 mulanto chilies, 4 ancho chilies, 4 pasilla chiles, and 4 chilpote chilies. There is a note warning the reader to be careful with the chilpotes, as they can "lift your head off." In any case, I simply can't get the stuff to cook the recipe—unless it is available to me under another name, which is entirely possible with peppers. And I have to ask whether four kinds of chili peppers are really necessary, or whether these Mexican dishes have gone the way of Texas chili, which can now include everything from shark belly to fire ants. Unless you are having Mexican gourmets for dinner, you can probably get by with only one kind of hot chili pepper in the recipe above. Who will know? If you've got Texans at the table, they are going to argue no matter what you do.

Anyhow, the recipe below for stuffed turkey contains only one kind of pepper—jalapeño, which is fairly easy to find in American markets.

The Stuffing
2 pounds ground pork or armadillo
2 tomatoes, chopped
1 medium onion, chopped
1 banana (firm, with greenish peel) or plantain
1 large or two small tart apples
¹/₄ cup raisins
2 jalapeño peppers, seeded and chopped
¹/₄ cup pecans
2 tablespoons peanut oil

Heat the peanut oil in a large skillet. Sauté the onion for a few minutes, then add and brown the pork, stirring with a wooden spoon. Pour off any excess fat. Stir in the banana, apple, raisins, tomatoes, pecans, and jalapeño peppers. (Be sure you have removed the seeds from these things, unless you want a hot stuffing.) Stir and simmer for a few minutes. Then let the mixture cool before stuffing the turkey.

Caution: Jalapeño juice can burn your eyes and even your hands. I don't wear rubber gloves when working with them, but I do proceed carefully. Never rub your eyes with your hand when working with jalapeños or other hot peppers.

The Bird
1 small wild turkey, 6 to 8 pounds
cheesecloth
melted butter or bacon drippings

Preheat the oven to 325 degrees. Fill the body cavity and the crop with the stuffing. Close and truss the bird. Put it breast side up on a rack in a baking pan of suitable size. Fold the cheesecloth and cut a double piece large enough to cover the bird's breast and legs. Soak the cheesecloth in melted butter or bacon drippings, then cover the bird. Insert a meat thermometer and put the baking pan in the center of the oven. Bake for about 2 hours, basting from time to time with melted butter or pan drippings, or both. Cook until the meat thermometer reads 180 degrees.

Remove the bird from the oven and cool a little before carving. Most of us will want to put the bird on a platter and carve it at the table. In any case, while the bird is cooling down, make the gravy.

The Gravy
all-purpose white flour
pan drippings
$1/2$ cup white wine
$1/2$ cup turkey stock or chicken stock

Pour the pan drippings into a skillet and heat. Slowly stir in a little flour to thicken the mixture. Mix the wine and stock, then pour it slowly into the gravy, stirring as you go. Simmer and stir until you have the gravy just the way you want it. Serve the gravy over pieces of carved turkey and dressing.

Fajitas

I don't know whether the fajita originated in Mexico or in the Southwest. In any case, it seems to fit nicely into this chapter. Fortunately, refrigerated tortillas are now available in many American supermarkets, or you can make you own if you are so inclined. I normally make these fajitas from strips of turkey breast, but the meat from a boned thigh can also be used. For best results, cut the meat into strips about ¼ inch thick. The meat slices more easily if it is partly frozen.

> 1 pound turkey meat, cut into thin strips
> 6 large flour tortillas
> 2 tablespoons cooking oil
> juice of 3 limes
> 1 jalapeño pepper
> 2 cloves garlic, crushed
> 1 tablespoon chopped cilantro
> 1 can green chilies (4-ounce size), chopped
> salt and freshly ground pepper
> toppings of your choice (see text below)

Warm the tortillas and cover with a damp cloth or put them into a tortilla bowl so that they stay warm and soft. Cut jalapeño pepper in half lengthwise and carefully remove the seeds and pith. Discard these and wash your hands. Then mince the jalapeño and garlic. Mix the lime juice, salt, black pepper, jalapeño, cilantro, and garlic. Put the turkey pieces into a nonmetallic container, pour the meat sauce over it, and marinate at room temperature for about an hour. Heat the oil in a skillet and sauté the turkey strips for 3 or 4 minutes on high heat. Add the can of green chilies and the liquid from the can to the skillet. Spoon the turkey mixture into the tortillas, top with your choice of condiments, and roll the tortillas. (You can also spoon some of the toppings beside the rolled tortillas if you choose.) Eat warm.

Toppings: Sour cream, salsa (see recipe in chapter 10), chopped avocado or guacamole, refried beans, shredded cheddar, chopped onions, shredded iceberg lettuce, and so on.

Turkey Castillane

This dish is popular in Mexico these days and is believed to have been brought there by the Spanish. But I must point out that the

Spanish got the tomato and peppers from Mexico. In any case, it can be made with wild turkey instead of chicken. You'll need about 3 pounds of bone-in thighs and legs, or about 2 pounds of pure meat.

> 3 pounds turkey thighs and legs
> 2 cups turkey or chicken stock
> 2 large tomatoes, chopped
> 1 large onion, diced
> 1 green bell pepper, diced
> 1/2 red bell pepper, diced
> 1/4 cup chopped parsley or cilantro
> 3 cloves garlic, minced
> 1/4 cup seedless raisins
> 1 cup dry white wine
> 2 tablespoons butter
> salt and pepper
> 3 cups cooked rice (cooked separately)
> pimento, diced
> water

The onion, peppers, and pimento should be cut into pieces about 1/4 inch in size. The tomatoes can be of a larger dice.

Put the turkey pieces into a stove-top Dutch oven. Sprinkle with salt and pepper, then barely cover with water. Bring to a boil, reduce heat, cover, and simmer for an hour, or until the turkey is tender. Remove the turkey pieces and pull the meat off the bone. Cut the meat into bite-size pieces. Discard the bones, but save the broth.

Melt the butter in a skillet. Sauté the onion and bell pepper for about 5 minutes, then stir in the parsley and garlic. Back to the Dutch oven. Measure out 2 cups of the broth, or add enough water to make 2 cups if you are short. Bring the 2 cups of broth to a boil, then add the contents of the skillet, along with the turkey, tomatoes, wine, and raisins. Bring to a new boil, reduce heat, and simmer for about 20 minutes, stirring as you go. (If necessary, thicken with a little cornstarch mixed in water.)

Put the rice in the center of a serving platter and pour the turkey mixture over it. Sprinkle the chopped pimento over the top.

Wild Turkey Tamales

In addition to making a convenient wrap, corn shucks add flavor to food. You can use fresh corn shucks, or boil or steam dried shucks. (I prefer to simmer them in broth.) If you don't have your own, you can purchase dried shucks in the Mexican foods section of most supermarkets. If you prepare your own, it's best to square off the ends so that all the shucks are the same size. For the measures below, you'll need about 25 shucks of normal size.

The Broth
bony pieces from turkey (neck, wings, rib cage)
water to cover
1 medium onion, chopped
salt and pepper to taste
1 bay leaf
$1/4$ cup chopped celery tops or cilantro

Put the bony pieces into a pot of suitable size, cover with water, and add the other ingredients. Bring to a boil, cover tightly, reduce heat, and simmer until the meat is falling off the bony parts. Strain out the bay leaf and other solids. (Pull all the meat from the bones and save it.)

If you are working with dry corn shucks, add them to the broth, bring to a boil, remove from heat, and soak for 2 hours.

The Mesa
2 cups finely ground cornmeal or masa harina
2 tablespoons shortening
1 teaspoon salt
turkey broth

In a bowl, mix the fine cornmeal and salt with enough broth to form a soft dough. (Before starting, however, measure out $1/4$ cup of broth for use below; also remove the corn shucks, letting them drain.) Add hot water if you run out of broth. Let the dough stand for about 15 minutes, then add a little more hot broth or water if needed.

The Meat

2 cups finely chopped turkey
2 tablespoons chili powder
1 medium onion, minced
2 cloves garlic, minced
1 teaspoon salt
$1/2$ teaspoon red pepper
$1/4$ cup stock or broth (see above)

Spread out the chopped turkey. Mix the red pepper, salt, and chili powder, then sprinkle this mixture over the turkey. Then mix in the onion, garlic, and broth.

Spread out a few of the corn shucks on a flat surface and place 1 tablespoon of the meat mixture in the center of each. Roll the shucks, then tie off the ends neatly with cotton twine. (Some people fold over the ends, but I prefer the twine to make the tamales hold together better.) When all of the tamales have been wrapped, rig for steaming.

A bamboo steamer works fine if you have one, or you can make a steamer by putting a rack in the bottom of a stock pot. Then stand the tamales on end. If you have a two-burner oblong pan of some sort, rig a rack on the bottom and place the tamales on it lengthwise. I often use a deep fryer designed to fit atop a stove-top grilling unit. In a pinch, try carrots, celery stalks, venison ribs, or other bones. When you have made the rack, pour in the broth before loading the tamales. Bring to a broil, cover tightly, reduce heat, and simmer for about 45 minutes, or until the shuck and tamale dough separate easily.

If you're in a cooking mood, double or triple the measures above. Then freeze the tamales for later use. A couple of minutes in a microwave heats them up just right. Leave the shucks on during the freezing, but if you plan to keep them very long it may be a good idea to wrap them again in plastic film. Use aluminum foil only if you plan to heat them in a regular oven.

Note: This recipe can also be made with a mixture of ground turkey and ground pork, or perhaps ground armadillo. The native Mexicans and Indians of Central and South America made extensive use of the armadillo not only for meat but also for its fat, which they used for cooking, just as the white man used lard from hogs. At the time of this writing, I've got a couple of armadillos rooting around in my yard at night. They had better watch their step.

Bonus eating: Save the leftover broth. Add the meat from the bony pieces and 1 can Rotel or stewed tomatoes. Eat as a soup. Dilute the broth with water if it is too rich for you.

Turkey Tacos

There are three basic ways to prepare tacos. In the United States, most of us simply buy preformed hard taco shells in the Mexican foods section of the supermarket and stuff them with suitable fillings. In Mexico, they are usually made from a flat, soft tortilla, which is rolled around the filling. It can then be eaten soft or it can be fried until it is crispy. I feel that either of these last two methods makes a taco that is much easier to eat than a stuffed shell. In any case, the recipe below is for a rolled and fried taco made with small corn tortillas. These are available under refrigeration (or frozen) in most supermarkets, or you can make your own from fine-ground whole kernel cornmeal or from *masa harina*. The fillings below are designed for an easy mix, and you can add to the recipe if you choose to do so. You can use the salsa recipe in chapter 10, or you can purchase salsa at the supermarket. (Most of the salsa will be bottled or canned, but you can sometimes find it freshly made and refrigerated.)

> 2 cups chopped cooked turkey
> 2 cups chunky salsa
> 1 cup shredded sharp cheddar
> finely grated cheddar
> 12 corn tortillas (soft)
> 3 strips bacon
> salt and black pepper

Fry the bacon in a large skillet until crisp and crumble it. Mix the turkey chunks, bacon, salt, and black pepper. Put about ¼ cup of the turkey mixture on each tortilla. Add about the same amount of salsa. Sprinkle with shredded cheese. Roll the tortillas and pin shut with round toothpicks. Heat the bacon grease, and fry the tortillas until they are brown and crisp on all sides. Sprinkle lightly with grated cheese. Eat while hot.

Notes: If you don't want the bacon grease, use a little vegetable oil for frying the tacos. Or forget about frying and merely steam the tacos for a few minutes. Remember that for easy variations you can purchase canned salsa in hot, mild, and so-so.

Wild Turkey in Grape Juice

In some parts of the world, cooking in grape juice is as common as cooking in wine. People who grow their own grapes, or who have access to wild grapes, as I do, might remember this fact. Also, you don't have to wait until the grapes are ripe; the juice of green grapes is used in the Caucasus to impart a tart but pleasant taste to meats.

The recipe below comes from Argentina, a country that grows huge grapes in Mendoza and, though it may not have wild turkeys, does have another large bird: the rhea, which at one time was widely hunted with the aid of bolas. I don't have a rhea or Mendoza grapes, but I have tried the recipe with a very large grape that grows in the southeastern United States, the scuppernong, as well as its cousin the bullace, or bullage. Both of these are muscadine grapes, and the bullace grows wild in great plenty in river and creek bottom lands. Of course, any good eating grape can be used.

I might add that domesticated turkeys are eaten in Argentina, and gobblers are often purchased live for home consumption. They are fed rum until they strut and gobble before they are led to the chopping block. The rum is believed to make the bird tender.

> wild turkey breast
> 1 pound of grapes (see note below)
> 4 tablespoons butter
> parsley
> salt and white pepper (optional)

Put the grapes into a suitable container and squeeze all the juice from them. Skin the turkey breast and fillet out both sides. Heat the butter and parsley in a skillet. Sauté the turkey breast fillets for about 10 minutes, turning once, until the pieces are lightly browned on both sides. Put the fillets into a saucepan of suitable size, and pour the butter and parsley over them. Pour in the grape juice. You should have enough juice to cover (barely) the turkey. If not, add a little water or squeeze out some more grapes. Bring to a light boil, decrease the heat to low, cover tightly, and simmer for an hour or so, or until the turkey is tender. Serve the breast on a small platter, and pour a little of the pan juice over it. The rest of the juice can be served in a bowl. It can also be thickened with flour or cornstarch.

Remember also that a wonderful pie can be made from the scuppernong or bullace hulls.

Note: Exact measures for the grapes required will depend on the size of the turkey breast and on the type of grapes that you use. A pound of small wild fox grapes, for example, will not yield as much juice as some other kinds of grapes.

FOUR

Grilled and Broiled Turkey

As a rule, fatty meat such as pork or well-marbled beef or Spanish mackerel is easier to grill than lean meats such as venison or walleye fillets or wild turkey. Yet, wild turkey is one of the best meats for the grill, provided it is not overcooked. Experience and confidence are the best guide, and, of course, it is impossible to give foolproof directions in a book, simply because so much depends on the heat of the fire, the distance from the meat to the fire, and the thickness of the meat. If in doubt, it's always best to cut into a piece of grilled turkey before serving it. When done, the meat is white. When raw, it is slightly translucent.

I often grill fingers cut from the breast of a turkey, and I *always* cut one of the thicker pieces in half when I believe it to be done. If it is not white all the way through, I put the halves back together and grill the batch a while longer, checking the center of the cut piece every 2 minutes or so.

Most of the recipes for grilling refer to cooking the meat, usually on a rack, directly over a source of heat—charcoal, wood coals, gas burner, or electrical element. (Anything cooked in a skillet is not broiled or grilled, in my opinion, although it might be *called* "pan broiled" or grilled.) True broiled meat is cooked under a source of heat, usually the top heating element of a kitchen oven. Many of the recipes for grilling will work reasonably well for broiling, especially the turkey fingers that have been marinated in a hot sauce, such as the *piripiri* recipe below. But grilling is more fun, and basting is much easier when the meat is on a grill instead of under a broiler.

All in all, I'll have to say that I enjoy grilling turkey more than any other way of preparing it. It's just more fun than sticking a bird into an oven and roasting it for hours. Be sure to try some of the following recipes.

Turkey with Piripiri Sauce

Grilled poultry, meat, and seafoods with a baste of a hot sauce called *piripiri* is very popular in Mozambique and several other parts of Africa. For red meat, the sauce contains lemon juice. For poultry, it contains coconut milk instead of lemon juice. I am fond of grilling fingers from the breast of American wild turkey by the recipe. Remember that coconut milk is not the juice from the center of a coconut. Instead, it is made by steeping shredded coconut meat in hot water, then squeezing out the milk. You can purchase coconut milk in some outlets or by mail order, or you can make your own by following the directions given in chapter 10.

Be warned that this recipe is quite hot.

> 2 or 3 pounds of turkey breast
> 1 cup coconut milk
> 1/2 cup butter
> 2 tablespoons chopped fresh parsley
> 3 cloves garlic, crushed
> 2 teaspoons cayenne pepper (or ground hot peppers)
> salt to taste

Cut the turkey breast with the grain into long strips about 3/4 inch thick. Put the strips into a nonmetallic container and cover them with a marinade made by mixing the coconut milk, pepper, garlic, and parsley. Marinate at room temperature for 2 hours. When you are ready to cook, build a good charcoal fire and let it burn down to coals. Drain the turkey pieces, reserving the marinade. Melt the butter and mix into the marinade, making a basting sauce.

Grease the grill lightly, then, using tongs, dip each turkey finger into the marinade and place it onto the grate, which should be about 4 inches from the heat. Turn the turkey from time to time, basting on each turn. (After about 5 minutes, sprinkle both sides of the turkey lightly with salt. I like crushed sea salt on mine.) Cook for a total of about 10 minutes, or until the turkey looks done on the outside. Then cut into a piece. It should be moist, should not run with pink juice, and should be white all through.This is a hot dish, so serve it with an ice cold drink, plenty of fluffy rice, and vegetables or salad, or even a chilled soothing melon.

Variations: Of course, you can grill the turkey fingers on an electric or gas grill, indoors or on the patio. I like the convenience of my stove-top grill, but I really prefer to flavor a charcoal fire with a few pieces of green hickory wood on it. I also grill on coals from a wood fire, which may be the best of all for flavor and atavistic satisfaction. With this in mind, consider grilling turkey fingers in camp. The marinade can be mixed at home and carried along in a jar, and you can substitute bacon drippings for the butter.

If you've got the time, you can grill whole turkey breasts, as well as thighs, with the recipe and technique. Just cook for a longer time on lower heat, so that the inside will get done before the outside burns.

Grilled Turkey Halves I

Although I don't recommend cooking a whole wild turkey over direct heat on a grill, or under it in a broiler, unless you have a rotisserie or a spit, you can do a great job on young birds if you cut them in half lengthwise or quarter them. The hard part, as with chicken halves, is in getting the inside done without burning the outside. Exact cooking times are not set forth below simply because too much depends on the heat, the thickness of the turkey, and the distance from the meat to the heat. An expert patio chef will know these things, but it is always safest to test the bird by cutting down to the bone before serving it. Don't cut too often, however; you'll lose the juice. The key to success is to grill the bird about 8 inches above low heat. A small turkey will usually take about 1 hour. Add some green or water-soaked wood chips to your fire if you want more smoke flavor.

1 small turkey, plucked and cut in half
1 cup melted butter
juice of 3 lemons (used separately)
2 cloves garlic, crushed
lemon-pepper seasoning salt

Mix a basting sauce of melted butter, juice of 2 lemons, and crushed garlic. Build a charcoal or wood fire or heat up the gas grill. Squeeze the juice from the third lemon and coat the bird halves on both sides. When the coals are ready, grease the rack and place the turkey halves on it. Turn after about 10 minutes, and baste the top lightly with the butter sauce. Then sprinkle lightly with lemon-pepper. Turn, baste, and sprinkle every 10 minutes or so until the turkey is almost done. (Remember that you'll need to cook the bird for about 1 hour. If the outside seems to be browning too quickly, decrease the heat or elevate the rack if it is adjustable.) Then turn every 5 minutes until the bird is ready to serve. Test for doneness by cutting into the thigh, going all the way to the bone.

Grilled Turkey Halves II

This recipe is similar to the one above except that it's hotter. It works best with a young bird. If you are cooking only half of the bird, or only breast fingers, cut the measures below in half. Before proceeding, make sure that your grill is long enough for half a turkey. If you have a small, circular grill, consider cutting the bird into quarters.

1 turkey split in half lengthwise
1 cup olive oil
2 tablespoons Louisiana hot sauce (or Tabasco)
2 tablespoons black pepper
juice of 3 lemons
$^1/_2$ tablespoon salt

Cut the bird in half lengthwise and put it into a suitable container, such as an enameled baking pan. Mix the other ingredients well and pour them over the turkey halves, making sure that all sides are well coated. Marinate for 2 or 3 hours. When you are ready to cook, build a fire in an oblong grill or turn on your electric grill. (I often use a stove-top grill for cooking half a small turkey.) Grease the grill's rack. Remove the bird from the marinade and place it on the rack. It's best to cook the turkey halves rather slowly. With charcoal, use a medium fire and elevate the bird 8 inches or so above it. With a stove-top grill, turn the thermostat down to mid-range. Turn the turkey halves and baste every 10 minutes. The bird should be done in about 1 hour. If in doubt, cut into a piece before serving.

With turkey fingers, the cooking time must be reduced drastically. When done to perfection, the fingers will be succulent and tender. If cooked too long, they will be dry and chewy.

Barbecued Wild Turkey

I use the term "barbecue" to indicate meat that has been cooked in one way or another and soused in a thick sauce, usually, but not always, with a tomato base. More often than not, I cook a barbecue on a grill, but many recipes can also be cooked in the oven or, better, in a pit in the ground. When grilling meat to be barbecued, as in this recipe, the secret is in cooking the meat slowly and using the sauce only toward the end of the cooking time. Using a thick sauce too early will result in a burnt sauce.

For the dish below, I use a whole turkey split in half, then grilled over direct heat (usually charcoal or wood coals) until it is done. This will usually take 1 hour or longer, but, of course, a good deal depends on the size of the bird, the heat of the fire, and the distance from the meat to the coals. Experience at the grill is the best guide. If in doubt, cut into the thick part of the thigh before using the thick sauce. If it is done, the juices will run clear and not pink.

The Bird
1 turkey, split in half
$^1/_2$ cup vinegar
melted butter
salt and pepper

The Sauce
1 cup catsup
1 cup honey
2 tablespoons powdered mustard
2 tablespoons candied ginger root, minced
1 medium onion, chopped
4 cloves garlic, minced

Mix all of the sauce ingredients in a saucepan and simmer for about 5 minutes. Pour into a basting pot and chill until cooking time. Build a fire in the grill and let it burn down to coals. While waiting for the coals, cut the turkey in half lengthwise and moisten all sides with vinegar. Grill the bird about 10 inches above moderate coals for about 30 minutes. Then baste with melted butter and sprinkle with salt and pepper. When the turkey is almost done, turn several times, basting with the barbecue sauce. When the bird is done, put it onto a long serving platter and top with any remaining sauce. Barbecued turkey goes with baked beans and thick potato chips (or potato salad) and garlic bread.

Turkey Teriyaki

There must be several thousand recipes for teriyaki, most of which call for broiling or grilling the meat, which may be pork, chicken, fish, duck, and so on. Turkey, too, can be cooked to advantage by this method. I prefer turkey breast cut into strips about 1 inch square, but boned thighs can also be used. In the recipe below, I have stuck to the basics for what I consider to be a classic teriyaki. A little brown sugar can also be added.

1^1/$_2$ or 2 pounds turkey breast strips
^{1}/$_2$ cup soy sauce
^{1}/$_2$ cup sake
^{1}/$_2$ tablespoon fresh grated ginger root

Mix a marinade with the soy sauce, sake, and grated ginger. Put the turkey strips into a nonmetallic bowl and pour in the marinade, tossing once or twice to coat all the turkey strips. Marinate at room temperature for about 3 hours. When you are ready to cook, build a hot charcoal fire in your grill, or heat up the gas or electric grill. Grill the meat about 4 inches from the heat, turning and basting several times with the leftover marinade. On my charcoal grill, 10 minutes is about right. I also cook this recipe on my stove-top electric grill, and this usually takes about 15 minutes. Since this recipe is prepared by direct heat without the aid of butter or fat, I take special precautions with it. I turn it often. Usually, I pile it up on the end of the grill, away from the direct heat, and let it sit for a few minutes before serving. This seems to ensure that the inside is done without drying the meat out too much.

In addition to grilling, the turkey can also be broiled in the oven. The cooking times will be about the same, provided that the broiling rack is about 5 inches from the source of the heat. I always broil meat with the oven door left open because I don't want to mix the broiling technique and baking. In any case, remember that turkey breasts tend to be dry and should not be cooked too long by direct heat.

Anyone who has a large covered grill may want to cook this recipe for a much longer time, using the indirect method and some wood chips. The idea, of course, is to put the charcoal on one side of the grill, along with a few wet wood chips or, better, some green wood blocks. Then put the meat on the other side of the grill. When using this method, turning the pieces is not necessary, but I do it anyway, once or twice, when I baste meat. The cooking times vary, depending on the fire, the size of your grill, and so on.

I usually serve this dish with rice and steamed vegetables.

Tabasco Turkey

I got this idea from a barbecue sauce recipe in a booklet called *What's Hot?* published by the McIlhenny Company of Avery Island, Louisiana, the Tabasco sauce folks. Although the sauce is used for wild turkey in this recipe, it can also be used for chicken or pork that is broiled or grilled. Be warned that it is hot stuff.

> turkey breast fingers
> $^1/_4$ cup prepared mustard
> $^1/_4$ cup unsulphured molasses
> $^1/_4$ cup vinegar
> 1 teaspoon Tabasco sauce
> $^1/_2$ teaspoon salt

In a bowl, stir together all of the ingredients except the turkey, making a sauce. Put the turkey fingers into a large bowl, pour 2 tablespoons of the sauce over the meat, and stir or toss to coat all sides. Leave at room temperature for 30 minutes. Preheat the oven broiler and adjust the rack to about 6 inches from the heat. Broil the turkey fingers for about 10 minutes on each side. Cut into a piece before serving. Ideally, the meat should be juicy but not reddish. Serve with plenty of green salad and cooling vegetables, and iced tea or cold water. In season, I also like this dish with vine-ripened tomatoes. This meat can also be grilled over charcoal, gas, or electric heat. I sometimes cook it on a stove-top grill.

Turkey with Indonesian Soy Sauce

This Indonesian recipe shows that not all food from the spice islands is highly seasoned. It does, however, taste rather strongly of soy sauce, which I happen to like. The recipe calls for Indonesian soy sauce, which is dark and strong, but I have cooked it with ordinary soy sauce found in American supermarkets.

> 1 wild turkey breast
> $^1/_2$ cup Indonesian soy sauce
> juice of 1 large lemon
> 2 cloves garlic, crushed
> 1 tablespoon peanut oil

Fillet the wild turkey breasts and cut the meat into fingers.

Put the meat into a nonmetallic bowl. Mix the other ingredients, pour over the turkey fingers, and toss to coat all sides. Marinate at room temperature for 3 or 4 hours, or overnight in the refrigerator. When you are ready to cook, build a charcoal fire and adjust the rack about 6 inches over the heat. Drain the turkey fingers, saving the marinade for a basting sauce. When the coals are ready, broil the fingers for 15 or 20 minutes, turning and basting every few minutes until the turkey is golden brown and tender.

I also cook this recipe on a stove-top grill or under a broiler in the oven. It is also excellent when stir-fried. As a variation, add lots of freshly ground black pepper.

Grilled Turkey Fingers with Garlic Sauce

Although this recipe can also be used for cooking half a turkey, or whole breast fillets, I like it best for grilling fingers. With a large chunk of meat, the grilling should be done by the indirect method; that is, a fire should be built on one side of a large covered grill, and the meat should be put on the other side. With grilled fingers, I like to put the meat close to the coals. The trick, of course, is to get the meat done on the inside without burning the outside. Pay constant attention to the meat, basting and turning each piece with tongs, and cut a piece in two to test for doneness before severing.

> turkey breast fingers, cut lengthwise about ³/₄ inch thick
> 1 cup olive oil
> 1 cup white-wine vinegar
> 10 cloves garlic, mashed
> 10 peppercorns, crushed
> 10 allspice berries, crushed
> Tabasco sauce
> bacon drippings or cooking oil

Put the olive oil and wine vinegar into a jar. Crush the peppercorns and allspice berries in a mortar and pestle (or by other

71

means) and put them into the jar with the oil and vinegar. Mash each garlic clove in the mortar and pestle or with the wide, flat blade of a chef's knife, and put the pulp into the jar. (You can also use a garlic press, but in my experience a chef's knife works better and is easier to find.) Add a few drops of Tabasco or other hot pepper sauce. Shake the jar and refrigerate it for at least a day before using. It will keep for a month or longer if refrigerated.

When you are ready to cook, build a hot fire in the grill. Brush the grate and the turkey fingers with bacon drippings. Grill about 4 to 6 inches above the coals, turning with tongs and basting with the garlic sauce from time to time. Serve hot with bread and vegetables of your choice. On the patio, I like to grill vegetables such as sliced eggplants and even sliced potatoes. For tailgating or grilling at a picnic, potato salad and coleslaw round out the meal, although I wouldn't rule out vegetables cooked in a "stir-fry" grilling basket.

Sesame Turkey

Here's an oriental way of grilling meat and then serving it with a sauce made from the marinade. Like most other oriental dishes, it should be served with lots of hot rice. I prefer to grill fingers from a turkey breast over charcoal or wood coals, but the meat can also be broiled or cooked atop an electric grill.

> 2 pounds wild turkey, cut into fingers
> 1 cup soy sauce
> 1 cup brown sugar
> $1/2$ cup sesame oil
> $1/2$ cup sesame seeds
> 2 tablespoon black pepper
> 10 green onions with half of tops, minced
> 10 cloves garlic, minced
> 1 tablespoon fresh ginger root, minced
> 2 tablespoons melted butter
> rice (cooked separately)

In a saucepan, mix and heat the soy sauce, brown sugar, sesame oil, sesame seeds, ginger, onions, garlic, and black pepper. Put the turkey fingers into a nonmetallic container and pour the soy mixture over them, tossing to coat all sides. Marinate at room temperature for 5 or 6 hours. When you are ready to cook, drain the meat and grill it over charcoal until done. Do not overcook. While the meat is grilling, heat the remaining marinade and simmer until thickened. When you turn the meat, baste it a couple of times with the melted butter. When the meat is done, put it onto a serving platter. Mix any remaining melted butter into the marinade mixture. Put the mixture into a bowl and serve over the grilled turkey and rice.

I usually cook this dish with fingers of breast meat, but I have also used boned leg quarters successfully, as well as wings.

Grilled Turkey Strip Steaks

To make these "strip steaks," I normally cut the turkey breast lengthwise into fingers about 1 inch thick. Then I put each finger between layers of waxed paper and pound them down with a meat mallet to a thickness of $1/2$ inch. For uniform cooking, it is important that all the fingers be almost exactly the same thickness.

> 2 pounds turkey breast strip steaks
> 2 tablespoons olive oil
> 3 cloves garlic, minced
> 1 teaspoon crushed dried oregano
> salt and freshly ground black pepper

Prepare the steaks as directed above and put them into a nonmetallic container. Mix the other ingredients and pour over the turkey, toss, and marinate for 30 minutes at room temperature. Build a medium hot charcoal fire. Remove the turkey steaks and drain. Grill for 3 or 4 minutes on each side. Do not overcook. Serve with Greek bread and a mound of Greek salad topped with feta cheese.

Good Ol' Boy Turkey Kabobs

A number of jackleg patio chefs around the country have gotten into the lazy habit of using Zesty Italian dressing for marinating turkey, chicken, and fish before broiling it. They often wrap a chunk of meat with half a strip of bacon before grilling it, a practice that I highly recommend to anyone who is apt to cook turkey too long. The mushrooms are also ideal for grilling, because exact cooking times aren't too critical.

> turkey breast
> Zesty Italian dressing
> bacon
> whole mushrooms
> crushed garlic (optional)
> salt and pepper to taste

Cut the turkey breast into kabob-size chunks. Put the meat into a nonmetallic bowl and pour some Zesty Italian dressing over it. Stir in some crushed garlic if you want it. (I often buy finely chopped garlic packed in oil, which is very easy to use and keeps for a long time in the refrigerator.) Toss to coat all sides of the meat. Marinate at patio shade temperature while you have a beer or two. Build a good charcoal fire or heat up the gas or electric grill. Wrap each piece of turkey in half a strip of bacon and stick it onto a skewer, alternating with whole mushrooms. Place the kabob about 6 inches over the heat. Turn and baste every 5 minutes or so until the bacon looks ready to eat. With thick bacon, this may take up to 30 minutes. During the last 5 minutes, sprinkle lightly with salt and pepper. If you have used chunks of turkey on the thick side, it's best to cut a piece in half to check for doneness before serving to your guests.

This recipe is also a good one for cooking in camp, especially if you are skilled enough to bag a turkey and knowledgeable enough to gather safe-to-eat fresh mushrooms.

Turkish Kabobs

The kabob may have originated in Turkey or nearby. Of course, the dish wasn't originally made with American turkey, but it was no doubt made with bustards, pheasants, and other game birds.

> breast of a small turkey
> ½ cup olive oil
> 4 cloves garlic, minced
> juice of 1 lemon
> salt and white pepper

Cut the turkey into bite-size pieces and put them into a non-metallic container. Mix the other ingredients and pour over the turkey. Marinate at room temperature for at least 2 hours. When you are ready cook, build a charcoal fire or heat up the gas or electric grill. Thread the turkey chunks onto skewers and grill for about 10 minutes, or until the turkey is done. Turn from time to time and baste with leftover marinade while cooking to prevent the meat from drying out. Do not overcook.

Island Turkey Kabobs

Here's a recipe that I like to cook on my stove-top grill. It can also be cooked over a charcoal or gas grill.

> 2 pounds turkey breast
> 3 tablespoons rum
> 1 tablespoon Creole mustard
> 2 tablespoons honey
> 1 tablespoon brown sugar
> 2 tablespoons olive oil
> 10 allspice berries, ground

Cut the turkey into chunks about 1½ inches thick. Put the

meat into a nonmetallic container. Mix the other ingredients and pour over the turkey pieces, tossing to coat all sides. Marinate at room temperature for 1 hour. When you are ready to cook, build a hot fire or preheat the electric or gas grill. Thread the turkey onto skewers and grill over medium hot coals, turning several times, for 10 to 15 minutes, or until the turkey pieces are brown and done.

FIVE

Skillet Specialties

Many cooks who really know their craft enjoy baking breads. They like to work the dough with their hands, saying that it feels alive and growing under their care. Others are patio chefs, who enjoy the fire and the grilling and the basting. Still others are skillet shakers, and I have to count myself among them. But I'm not too fancy and certainly not skilled enough to toss the contents into the air, although I do sometimes shake the skillet quite a bit to keep food from sticking or to keep the gravy from separating. It's a hands-on kind of cooking.

My favorite skillet is an old 10-inch cast-iron model, but I also use larger ones for some recipes. If properly cared for, cast iron is the original no-stick material. But other materials can also be used. Aluminum is satisfactory, provided the metal is thick. There are also some good modern skillets made from metal and coated with some sort of hard substance. Again, these should be thick in order to work well—and be warned that these are likely to crack and peel under high heat. Electric skillets work nicely for most purposes, but I've never cared too much for them.

In any case, all the recipes in this chapter can be made with a simple skillet. Fried turkey was treated in chapter 1, and a few other skillet recipes appear in other chapters. Many skillet cooks insist on stirring with a wooden spoon. I am one of these, but the reasoning is difficult to defend. Wooden spoons just seem to work better, and don't scrape so noticeably on the metal bottom of the skillet when you stir your roux or gravy.

Wild Turkey Jambalaya

This recipe makes a rather bland dish by Cajun standards, but of course, a good deal depends on how many shakes you give that bottle of Tabasco sauce. I like to make jambalaya from turkey breast, but thigh meat can also be used. It's best if you'll fillet the breast, or bone the thigh, and then cut the meat into chunks about 1 inch square. I also like the cured ham cut to about the same dimensions, or perhaps a little smaller.

> 2 pounds cubed turkey
> $\frac{1}{2}$ pound cubed smoked or cured ham
> 4 strips bacon
> 1 large onion, diced
> 1 rib celery with green tops, diced
> 1 green bell pepper, diced
> 1 pound fresh or canned tomatoes, diced
> $\frac{1}{2}$ cup chopped fresh parsley
> 3 cloves garlic, minced
> 2 bay leaves
> $\frac{1}{2}$ teaspoon salt
> $\frac{1}{4}$ teaspoon dry thyme
> $1\frac{1}{2}$ cups long-grain rice
> $1\frac{1}{2}$ cups water

Fry the bacon in a large, heavy-duty skillet about 13 inches in diameter. (If you don't have one that large, try a stove-top Dutch oven.) Remove the bacon and drain it on a brown bag. In the bacon drippings, quickly brown the turkey and ham, onion, pepper, and celery. Add the water, bay leaves, and crumbled bacon. Simmer for 30 minutes. Add the chopped tomatoes, garlic, salt, parsley, and thyme. Bring to a boil. Add the rice. Bring to a new boil, then reduce the heat and simmer for 30 minutes. Stir from time to time and add a little water if needed. Serve in bowls with good French bread.

Variations: Although the word *jambalaya* implies ham, I sometimes substitute smoked venison sausage. Also, I am fond of using a few strong wild onions and their green tops instead of garlic and parsley. Anyone lucky enough to have ramps on hand should surely try them.

Skillet Stir-Fry

A wok or a large skillet can be used to cook this recipe. It's best to proceed with the breast of a young, tender bird. Cut the breast across the grain into 1/4-inch strips. It helps to partly freeze the meat before cutting the strips. It also helps to have a sharp knife. The measures below will work for about 1 to 1 1/2 pounds of meat. I allow 1/4 pound per person.

> 1- to 1 1/2-pounds turkey breast, cut into strips
> 1 stalk celery
> 1 small green bell pepper
> 1 small red bell pepper
> 1 medium onion
> 1 can bean sprouts (16-ounce size)
> 1 can water chestnuts (5-ounce size)
> 1/2 cup chicken or turkey stock
> 2 tablespoons peanut oil
> 1 tablespoon sesame oil
> 2 tablespoons soy sauce
> 2 teaspoons cornstarch
> 2 slices fresh ginger root, 1/8 inch thick
> rice (cooked separately)

Get everything ready before starting the stir-fry. Slice the turkey as directed above. After removing the seeds and core from the green and red peppers, cut them into thin strips lengthwise. Cut the onion into 8 sections lengthwise. Slice the celery thinly on a diagonal. Drain the cans of bean sprouts and water chestnuts. Heat the peanut and sesame oils in the skillet until very hot. While heating, add the ginger root. When the oil is ready, fry the celery, green pepper, red pepper, and onion for 4 to 5 minutes. With a slotted stir-fry spoon, remove the vegetables and put them on a heated platter. (If you are using a very large skillet, pull part of it off the heat and elevate the end so that the oil runs down; push the vegetables to the high side.) Add the turkey strips to the oil and stir-fry for 4 to 5 minutes. Mix the sautéed vegetables with the turkey. Add the water chestnuts, bean sprouts, and turkey stock. Pour the soy sauce into a measuring cup and stir in the cornstarch. Gradually pour the cornstarch mixture into the skillet, stirring constantly. Heat and stir until the mixture thickens. Serve immediately with rice.

Turkey Marengo

I like to cook this famous dish in a large cast-iron jambalaya skillet, but a large electric skillet can also be used. I use either breast or boned thigh meat for this recipe, or a mixture of both. The meat is cut into serving-size pieces but should not be too thick.

> 3 pounds wild turkey
> 20 pearl onions or 12 shallots, whole
> 2 cloves garlic, chopped
> 8 ounces fresh mushrooms, shallot-size
> 1 can tomatoes (16-ounce size)
> $1/2$ cup dry sherry
> olive oil
> salt and pepper
> paprika
> rice (cooked separately)

Heat a little olive oil in the skillet. Sauté the mushrooms and onions for 5 minutes, then remove with a slotted spoon and set aside to drain. Add the turkey pieces to the skillet and sprinkle with paprika. Cook until the turkey is browned on all sides, turning occasionally. Add the tomatoes and juice from the can, sherry, garlic, salt, and pepper. Bring to a light boil, reduce heat, cover, and simmer for 30 minutes, or until the turkey is tender. Stir from time to time and add a little more salt and pepper if needed. Serve with rice.

Wild Turkey Cacciatore

George Leonard Herter, of the old Herter's mail-order house in Minnesota, once argued that the great Italian dish called *cacciatore*, meaning hunter's stew, was taken to that country from America by immigrants going back to the homeland. He has a point, since most of the recipes for this dish call for ingredients that were unknown in Europe before the New World was discovered. Tomatoes and bell peppers, which are necessary in most recipes called cacciatore, are American. So is allspice. Since the New World had no chickens or pheasants, the original was probably made with the wild turkey. If you want to go all-American, use peanut oil instead of olive oil and use a native brew, such as spruce beer or pulque, instead of Chianti or other vino, and use a crushed chili pepper instead of the black pepper. Anyhow, an excellent cacciatore can be made as follows.

> 4- or 5-pound young wild turkey
> 2 pounds tomatoes (canned will do), chopped
> 1 can tomato sauce (8-ounce size)
> 2 bell peppers, chopped
> 1 large onion, chopped
> 4 or 5 cloves garlic, minced
> 1/2 cup olive oil
> 1 cup Chianti or other wine
> salt and pepper to taste
> 1/2 teaspoon crushed allspice
> 2 bay leaves
> 1/2 teaspoon crushed thyme

Cut the bird into pieces. In a large skillet (about 13 inches in diameter) or a stove-top Dutch oven, heat the olive oil (or peanut oil) and lightly brown the turkey pieces. Drain. In the remaining oil, sauté the onions, bell peppers, and garlic for 4 to 5 minutes, stirring with a wooden spoon. Add the wine and tomato sauce. Fit in the browned turkey pieces, then add the tomatoes (and the juice if using canned), salt, pepper, bay leaves, allspice, and thyme.

Bring to a light boil, reduce heat, cover tightly, and simmer for 1 hour, adding a little water if needed. Before serving, check whether the turkey pieces are tender. It not, cook longer, adding water if needed. Remember that the drumsticks have lots of tendons and are therefore difficult to eat, so make sure that your guest of honor gets a piece of breast or a thigh.

Turkey with Noodles

I normally use turkey breast for this recipe, but thigh meat can also be used. In either case, bone the meat and cut it into 1-inch cubes. The measures below work for a 12-inch skillet. If you want to double the recipe, try a stove-top Dutch oven.

> 1 to 1½ pounds turkey
> 1 medium onion, chopped
> 8 ounces fresh mushrooms, sliced
> 2 tablespoons butter
> ½ cup sour cream
> Hungarian paprika
> salt and pepper to taste
> chopped fresh parsley
> egg noodles, cooked separately (5-ounce package)
> ½ cup water

Cut the turkey meat into cubes, then sprinkle it lightly with pepper and about ½ teaspoon paprika. (It's easier to merely sprinkle some paprika out of the top of the can without measuring.) Heat the butter in a skillet, then sauté the turkey cubes for about 5 minutes. Pour off excess butter. Add the water and heat to a boil. Reduce heat, cover, and simmer for at least 30 minutes, or until the turkey is tender. In a smaller skillet, heat a little more oil and sauté the onion and mushrooms for about 5 minutes, stirring as you go. Add the onion and mushrooms to the turkey. Stir and cook for about 5 minutes. Then stir in the sour cream and more paprika. Heat for a few minutes, stirring, but do not allow to boil. Serve the turkey over egg noodles (cooked according to the directions on the package), and sprinkle each serving lightly with chopped parsley. Serves from 3 to 5, depending on their appetites and capacity.

Note: This recipe is very similar to stroganoff. Any stroganoff recipe that calls for chicken can be used to advantage with turkey.

Skillet Turkey Fingers

I highly recommend this recipe for wild turkey if you've got a young and tender bird. It's easy to cook, and is very good.

> 1 to 2 pounds turkey breast fingers
> 1/2 cup white-wine Worcestershire sauce
> 3/4 cup butter
> 1 medium onion, minced
> 1/2 tablespoon minced fresh parsley
> salt and white pepper

Skin the turkey breast and cut it into finger-size pieces. Heat the butter in a large skillet. Salt and pepper the fingers lightly, then sauté them for 4 to 5 minutes, or until they are nicely browned and cooked through. Do not overcook. Remove the fingers, drain, and keep warm. In the remaining hot butter, sauté the minced onion and parsley for 2 to 3 minutes. Stir in the white-wine Worcestershire sauce and simmer for 2 to 3 minutes to make a sauce. Turn off the heat. Put the turkey fingers onto a warm serving platter and pour the sauce over them.

This recipe is always good with mashed potatoes and steamed asparagus or boiled vegetables. The last batch that I cooked went very nicely with some stir-fried vegetables, to which I added a little of the sauce.

Turkey Sauce Piquante

This Cajun dish is very good when cooked with turkey, and it's easy to cook in a large skillet. I normally make it with breast meat, but boned thighs can also be used. I always cut the meat into serving-size portions. "Cajun tomatoes" refers to spiced tomatoes that are sold in cans. You can also use "Rotel tomatoes," which are on the hot side. If you can find neither of these, use a can of regular tomatoes and a little Tabasco sauce.

> 2 pounds turkey pieces
> 1 large onion, chopped
> 3 cloves garlic, minced
> 2 bell peppers, chopped
> 2 stalks celery, chopped
> 8 ounces fresh mushrooms, sliced
> 1 can tomato paste (6-ounce size)
> 1 can Cajun tomatoes (16-ounce size)
> 2 bay leaves
> 1 tablespoon minced fresh parsley
> salt and pepper to taste
> 2 tablespoons cooking oil
> rice (cooked separately)

Heat the cooking oil in a large skillet, then brown the turkey pieces on both sides. Remove the turkey and sauté the onion, peppers, celery, mushrooms, and garlic for a few minutes, until the onions turn clear. Put the meat back into the skillet. Increase the heat and add the tomato paste and canned tomatoes, along with the juice from the can. Stir in the parsley, salt, pepper, and bay leaves. Simmer slowly until the turkey is tender, adding a little water if needed. Serve over rice.

Note: I am fond of cooking this dish with wild onions and part of their green tops. When using these, I omit the garlic, onion, and parsley. Be warned, however, that some of the wild onions are on the strong side.

Murphy Norton Divan

I got this recipe from my mother-in-law—but don't tell her that I switched it from chicken to wild turkey and that I put some salt into the dish.

1 pound turkey breast
1 package frozen asparagus, thawed (12-ounce size)
1½ cups dry Minute rice
1 cup milk
½ cup mayonnaise
¼ cup water
¼ cup grated Swiss cheese
2 tablespoons butter or margarine
1 red bell pepper, seeded and cut into strips
1 chicken bouillon cube
salt and pepper

Cut the turkey breast into 1-inch chunks. Heat the butter in a skillet, and sauté the turkey pieces for about 5 minutes. Warm the milk and water, then dissolve the bouillon cube in it. Pour the liquid into the skillet. Add the asparagus, pepper strips, salt, and pepper. Bring to a full boil. Stir in the rice, cover, remove from the heat, and let stand for 5 minutes. Then stir in the mayonnaise and grated cheese.

Serve with vegetables and bread of your choice.

Wild Turkey and Swamp Cabbage

Swamp cabbage, the heart or the bud of the palm, was a popular vegetable with the Indians and the early settlers of Florida, South Carolina, and other states with suitable climate for growing palm and palmetto trees.

Not many years ago, the sportsman could gather his own swamp cabbage, or he could sometimes purchase it at country stores. If he had plenty of money, he could (and still can) purchase it in swanky restaurants. It can also be found in cans in the gourmet sections of some supermarkets. The canned product (called heart of palm) usually comes from Brazil or Central America. Wild-foods foragers who don't want to cut down a palm tree might choose to substitute Jerusalem artichokes, renewable tubers that can be gathered in the wild from a species of sunflower.

1¹/₂ pounds diced turkey breast
2 large fresh tomatoes, peeled and chopped
4 green onions with half of tops, chopped
4 cloves garlic, minced
1 ripe avocado
1 can heart of palm (16-ounce size)
2 tablespoons chopped cilantro or parsley
juice of 3 lemons
¹/₂ cup olive oil
salt and pepper to taste

Dice the turkey meat into 1-inch cubes. Heat the olive oil in a cast-iron skillet. Sauté the chopped green onions, cilantro, and garlic for 4 minutes. Add the diced turkey and stir-fry for 6 minutes, stirring with a wooden spoon. Add the chopped tomato, salt, pepper, and lemon juice; then cook for 4 to 5 minutes. Remove peel and dice the avocado, and cut the palm heart logs into wheels. Sprinkle lemon juice over the avocado and heart of palm, then stir these carefully into the turkey mixture. Serve over lettuce leaves along with generous chunks of hot buttered French bread or toasted garlic crackers. (I make the latter by spreading a little butter on ordinary saltines, then sprinkling them lightly with garlic powder and toasting them for a few minutes in the oven. These burn quickly, so check them frequently. Crackers that have lost crunch can be used.)

Blackened Turkey

The blackening technique got its start in Louisiana a few years ago with blackened redfish. It's not unusual these days to see blackened chicken, blackened venison, blackened pork, blackened duck, and so on. It is, however, unusual to see it done right. Most blackened chicken, for example, is merely highly seasoned pan-broiled chicken. To be perfectly honest, I think that everybody ought to try blackened meats just for the experience of it—but don't count on it. Serve it to your guests as a side dish.

The technique below for turkey will work with most other

meats. In order to keep it simple and short, I have listed a commercial blackening spice. Various brands are available in most supermarkets. Use your own mix if you prefer. It is necessary to have a cast-iron skillet or griddle simply because other materials will not hold up to the high temperatures required. It's also best to blacken outside the house on wood coals or perhaps real charcoal. (Most briquettes won't get hot enough.) Hard coal or oak wood makes a hot fire and is ideal.

> turkey slices
> blackening seasoning for poultry
> Hungarian paprika
> butter

Mix quite a bit of blackening seasoning half-and-half with mild Hungarian paprika. Slice the turkey breast into 1-inch cutlets. Put each cutlet between sheets of waxed paper, and beat them down to a thickness of $1/2$ inch. Build a hot fire, and put the skillet or griddle onto red-hot coals. Get the pan very hot. Do not put butter or oil on it. Melt the butter in a separate pan and quickly flip-flop each cutlet in it. Then coat each cutlet thickly with the spice mix. Using tongs, pick a fillet up by the edge and put it down onto the hot skillet. After a minute or so, turn the cutlet over and blacken the other side for 1 to 2 minutes. Put it onto a warm platter, and baste it with a little butter. Treat each piece of meat separately until you have cooked the whole batch. Serve with lots of cold salad, bread, and a goblet of iced beverage.

This is a good recipe to cook in camp, where there is plenty of fresh air to blow away the smoke. Most camp cooks are going to burn the meat anyway.

SIX

Stews and Soups

A good wild turkey stew is hard to beat for ordinary eating, and I am especially fond of turkey and dumplings on a cold day. Some of the recipes in this chapter make a complete meal if served with plenty of fresh bread and a hearty salad. The classic American Brunswick stew, for example, has plenty of fresh (or fresh-frozen) vegetables in it, as well as the meat. Also remember that the world's most famous turkey recipe, *Molé de Poblano de Guajolote*, covered in chapter 3, is essentially a stew. Another of my favorites has no classic name and requires only a short list of ingredients; this one (the last recipe in this chapter) is simply made with a turkey frame, ham bone, rice, and tomatoes.

Brunswick Stew

I have strong and mixed feelings about this dish. The original recipe, I think, was probably made with squirrels and rabbits, along with some fresh American vegetables. Gradually, people who wrote cookbooks left out the game and substituted chicken, a bird that was brought here from Europe, and canned vegetables. Now that frozen vegetables are readily available, I recommend them over the canned fare not only because of their better flavor, but also because they are not as mushy when cooked in this stew. Of course, the early settlers might well have used turkey along with the small game, and I allow it in the recipe. Although the list below calls for a whole wild turkey, you may want to save the breast for other recipes and make Brunswick stew from the legs, thighs, and bony parts, along with, perhaps, a squirrel, rabbit, or even a muskrat, if you are fortunate enough to have one. The exact amount of meat in the recipe isn't critical, so you can use pretty much what you've got, within reason. I also use ¹/₂ pound salt pork in the recipe, but anyone who has a problem with hog fat or salt can omit it entirely.

> 7- or 8-pound wild turkey
> ¹/₂ pound salt pork
> 6 cups water
> 1 package frozen baby lima beans (10-ounce size)
> 1 package frozen cut okra (10-ounce size)
> 1 package frozen whole kernel corn (10-ounce size)
> 1 large onion, chopped
> 2 large potatoes, diced
> 1 can tomatoes (16-ounce size) or 4 large fresh tomatoes
> salt and pepper
> 3 bay leaves

Dice the salt pork, brown it lightly in a skillet, and pour off most of the grease that cooks out of it. Add the chopped onions and sauté for a couple of minutes before turning off the heat.

Cut the turkey into pieces and put it, along with the giblets, into a large pot. Add the water and the bay leaves. Cover, bring to a boil, reduce heat, and simmer for about 40 minutes, or until the turkey is tender. Then take out the pieces, pull the meat from the bones, cut it into chunks, and return it to the pot. Actually, I start boning the turkey before the 40 minutes is up, working first with the smaller pieces.

When the meat is ready, discard the bay leaves, turn the heat to high, and add all the vegetables, along with the sautéed onion, diced salt pork, and salt to pepper to taste. Bring to a boil, cover, reduce heat, and simmer for 30 minutes. Toward the end, add a little water if needed to get the consistency that you like. If it's too soupy for your taste, leave the lid off during the last part of the cooking.

Serve Brunswick stew hot in bowls. Make a large batch and freeze some for future use. I like to put it into cup-size microwavable containers; then we can get out as many containers as we need for lunch.

Turkey Paella

This wonderful recipe is based on the classic Spanish dish. I make it with a small wild turkey or half a large wild turkey, along with venison sausage and assorted seafoods. (You can also breast a turkey for stir-fry or some other dish, then use what's left for this recipe. You can vary the seafoods, depending on what you've got on hand.) The crusty cheese top is not conventional, but it really sets this dish off, giving it eye appeal as well as taste.

> 1 small wild turkey (or part of a larger one)
> $1/2$ pound venison sausage, cut into 1/2-inch rounds
> $1/2$ pound shrimp in shells
> 2 dozen fresh oysters (with juice from shell)
> 2 dozen fresh clams (with juice from shell)
> 2 large onions, chopped
> 2 red bell peppers
> 4 cloves garlic, chopped
> 2 cups long-grain rice (uncooked)
> $1/2$ cup olive oil
> $1/2$ cup sherry
> 3 cups hot water with 3 chicken bouillon cubes
> freshly grated Parmesan cheese
> salt and pepper to taste
> $1/2$ teaspoon saffron

Disjoint the bird. Heat the olive oil in a large skillet and brown the pieces lightly. Put the turkey pieces into a large Dutch oven with a tight lid. Add the hot water, into which chicken bouillon cubes have been dissolved. Bring to a light boil, cover tightly, and simmer until the turkey is tender. (If you are using tough seafood, such as squid, conch, or octopus, add it to the pot with the turkey.) When the turkey is done, remove the pieces and pull off the meat in large chunks. Cut the red bell pepper into strips and sauté them for a few minutes, until tender and limp; strain these out and set aside to drain. Sauté the onions, garlic, and sausage for a few minutes in the skillet, adding a little more oil if needed. Then put the turkey chunks and onions back into the Dutch oven. Set the timer for 20 minutes and add the rice, bring to a bubble, reduce heat, and cover tightly. When the timer sounds off, add the shrimp, oysters, and clams and simmer for about 5 minutes, stirring in the saffron, wine, salt, and pepper. (The saffron is mostly for color. If you don't have it on hand, try turmeric or annatto.)

Heat the oven broiler. Place the strips of red pepper on top of the stew and sprinkle with grated Parmesan. Broil until the cheese melts and browns nicely. Serve in bowls with plenty of hot bread on the side, along with a green salad. Although paella is a Spanish dish, I like it with hot French bread and a huge Greek salad.

Turkey Noodle Soup

My mother-in-law swears that her chicken noodle soup will somewhat relieve the symptoms of a common cold and even the flu. Well, I say that my wild turkey noodle soup will help *anything* that you've got! I usually cook it with what's left of the bird after I fillet out both sides of the breast. The recipe takes several hours to prepare, and it's easier if you will prepare the stock a day ahead of your deadline.

The Stock
wild turkey leg quarters and frame
2 bay leaves
water

On day one, fillet the meat off both sides of the breastbone and save it for turkey fingers or some other suitable recipe. Remove the leg quarters and separate these into drumsticks and thighs. (There is no need to remove the skin or any fat that might be on the bird; the fatty parts add flavor to the stock and can be skimmed off later.) Put the pieces into a stove-top Dutch oven or other suitable pot. Barely cover with water and turn on the heat. Cut the back in half, or at least separate the rib section from the rest. Put these bony parts into the pot, fitting them in as best you can. (They don't have to be covered with water.) Add the bay leaves. Bring to a boil, reduce heat, cover tightly, and simmer for 2 to 3 hours, or until the turkey meat is tender. Turn off the heat. Take out the pieces and pull off the meat with a fork. Discard the bones and the skin. Cut the meat into chunks. Put the meat into a bowl of suitable size, cover it with plastic wrap, and refrigerate it. Put the stock from the pot into a suitable container and refrigerate it, too.

The Soup
4 cups turkey stock
4 ounces egg noodles
3 small Irish potatoes, peeled and diced
2 or 3 medium carrots, scraped and diced
2 stalks celery with green tops, chopped
1 large onion, chopped
1 cup what-ya-got
salt to taste
red pepper flakes

On day two, the stock will be cool and the fat will have risen to the top. You can remove it and throw it away if you don't want it. Discard the bay leaves.

Measure out 4 cups of stock and put it into the pot. (If you don't have 4 cups, add some water.) Add the chopped vegetables, noodles, and other ingredients. Bring to a boil, cover, reduce heat, and simmer for about 25 minutes, or until the potatoes and carrots are done. (I prefer mine not to be too mushy.) I think that crushed red pepper flakes give a good flavor to this soup, but in a pinch black pepper will do. While cooking our last batch of this soup, my wife sliced up a fresh green jalapeño pepper and put it, seeds and all, into the soup. This negated the need for red or black pepper and made the soup a little hot for some tastes. If you want the jalapeño flavor without all of the heat, remove the seeds (and wash your hands) before chopping up the pepper. (See the caution under Mexican Stuffed Turkey in chapter 3.)

The mystery ingredient called what-ya-got can be most any vegetable that you have on hand that needs to be used up right away. In our last batch, for example, my wife threw in two spears of semifresh asparagus and, over my objection, a handful of shredded purple cabbage. It was delicious. I wouldn't want too much purple cabbage in the soup, but with some what-ya-gots I'll allow more than 1 cup. Fresh mushrooms, for example.

Turkey and Mushroom Soup

I got this recipe from Euell Gibbons, who said in *Stalking the Wild Asparagus,* "This is one of the finest soups ever made by man, and yet, when cheap chicken parts are used, it costs next to nothing to make." I like it made with turkey back, wings, and drumsticks. Sometimes I'll use wild mushrooms, but more likely than not I'll use a package from the supermarket. Gibbons's recipe calls for monosodium glutamate, an ingredient whose popularity has pretty much come and gone. These days, I usually omit it. Here's the list for my version.

> turkey parts
> 16 ounces mushrooms, sliced
> 1 medium onion
> $1/2$ cup fresh celery leaves
> 4 tablespoons butter
> 2 tablespoons flour
> 1 teaspoon salt
> $1/8$ teaspoon freshly grated ginger
> 4 tablespoons sherry
> $1/2$ cup light cream
> freshly ground black pepper

Put the turkey parts into a large pot and cover with water. Add the onion and celery leaves, bring to a boil, reduce heat, cover, and simmer for 1 to 2 hours, or until the meat is tender and pulls easily from the bone with a fork. Remove the turkey pieces from the pot and pick off the meat. Strain out 1 quart of the pot liquid. (Discard the onion and celery, but save what's left of the liquid for other soups. If you don't have a full quart, add some water.)

In a skillet, melt the butter and sauté the mushrooms for about 20 minutes, or until they are tender. (Some of the wild mushrooms, such as the sulfur mushroom, *Polyporus sulphureus,* are tough and should be cooked for a much longer time.) Remove the mushrooms, letting them drain on a brown paper bag. To the butter and juice in the skillet, stir in the flour, salt, and ginger. Simmer and stir with a wooden spoon, as when making a roux, until you have a smooth paste. Add the turkey broth and turn up the heat. Stir in the turkey meat and the mushrooms. Heat through, then slowly stir in the sherry and light cream.

Serve in bowls, along with a pepper mill so that each person can season to taste. I insist on the pepper mill, or at least freshly ground black pepper, not only for the taste but also for the aroma. Serve with hot French bread.

Turkey and Groundnut Stew

The peanut is as American as baseball. The nut originated in Central or South America, where the turkey was first domesticated, and went from there to Africa during the slave trade. From there it came to Virginia. In North America, it became more of a snack than a staple food, but in Africa and parts of Asia the peanut became a part of the cuisine and is called groundnut, goober, pender, and ground pea. It is, as a matter of fact, a pea or legume instead of a nut. Since I was born and raised on a peanut farm, where we harvested 50 or 60 tons a year, I was surprised to learn that they are used in recipes in other lands. In fact, I laughed when I heard that peanut butter could be used to advantage in stews. I don't laugh anymore. Here is one of my favorite recipes, called *hkatenkwan*, a stew from Ghana, where it is made with chicken. I say it is better with the American wild turkey, and I have adapted the recipe from *The Africa News Cookbook.* I might add that African and many oriental cuisines also depend heavily on the American chili pepper.

turkey with breast meat removed
²/₃ cup peanut butter or ground roasted peanuts
2 cups fresh or frozen okra
1 medium eggplant, peeled and cubed
1 cup onion, chopped
¹/₂ whole onion
1 cup tomatoes, chopped
2 tablespoons tomato paste
2 hot chilies, crushed, or 1 teaspoon red pepper flakes
2 teaspoons salt
1-inch piece of ginger root
1 tablespoon peanut oil
2 cups water

Disjoint the turkey and put it into a large pot (black cast iron, of course) with the water, ginger root, and onion half. Bring to a boil, cover, reduce heat, and simmer. In another pot, heat the peanut oil and cook the tomato paste over low heat for 5 minutes. To the paste, add the chopped onion and tomatoes, cooking and stirring (with a wooden spoon, of course) until the onions are clear. Remove the turkey pieces from the other pot and put them, along with about half the broth, into the pot with the tomato paste. Add the peanut butter, salt, and peppers. Cook and stir for 5 minutes. Add the eggplant and okra. Cook until the chicken and vegetables are tender. One by one, fish out the turkey pieces and pull the meat from the bones. Discard the bones and add the meat back to the stew. Add more broth if needed, but remember that this is a stew, not a soup. Serve hot over rice.

Variation: The same recipe can also be used to make a soup, by adding 6 cups of water instead of 2.

Peking Turkey Chowder

The Chinese and the Japanese cook with flowers, and the chrysanthemum is one of the favorites. Provided that they are not overcooked, the petals have a slightly piquant flavor. They can be eaten raw in salads, or added to soups, stews, and other dishes. I don't know where the recipe below originated, but I found it in a book called *The Forgotten Art of Flower Cookery*, by Leona Woodring Smith. It calls for cooked turkey, which can be leftover or freshly boiled meat. I had made this recipe some time ago, and, while writing this book, I tried it with leftover baked wild turkey and with yucca blooms instead of chrysanthemum petals. It was wonderful. The recipe calls for 5 cups of turkey stock. Chicken stock may be substituted or, in a pinch, 5 cups of water and 5 chicken bouillon cubes.

> 2½ cups cubed cooked turkey
> 5 cups turkey stock
> 2 cups potatoes, diced
> 1½ cups whole kernel corn
> 1 cup chrysanthemum petals
> 1 cup light cream
> ¾ cup celery, chopped
> ½ cup onion, chopped
> 2 tablespoons green pepper, chopped
> 1½ tablespoons minced parsley
> 4 tablespoons butter
> pinch of tarragon
> salt and pepper to taste

Heat the butter in a pot of suitable size, and sauté the onion for about 5 minutes, until transparent. Add the green pepper, celery, potatoes, corn, turkey stock, and tarragon. Add salt and pepper to taste and cook gently for 15 minutes. Add the turkey and cream. Stir in the parsley and chrysanthemum petals, then remove the pot from the heat. Stir before serving. The chowder can be reheated if necessary.

Wild Turkey and Shrimp Gumbo

If you catch your own shrimp or have access to freshly caught shrimp, you're in business. If not, head for the nearest creek and catch a mess of fresh crayfish.

1 wild turkey breast, filleted
2 pounds peeled shrimp or crayfish tails
1 gallon water
6 pieces bacon
1 cup all-purpose flour
1 large onion, chopped
4 cloves garlic, minced
1 small stalk celery with tops, chopped
1 cup fresh or frozen okra, chopped
$1/2$ cup chopped fresh chives or green onion tops
$1/2$ cup chopped fresh parsley
3 bay leaves
salt and pepper to taste
rice (cooked separately)

In a large stove-top Dutch oven, brown the bacon. Remove the bacon and add the flour to the drippings. Lower the heat and stir for 5 or 10 minutes. Add the chopped onion, garlic, okra, celery, parsley, chives (or onion tops), bay leaves, salt, pepper, and half of the water. Stir and bring to heat. Cut the turkey breast fillets into chunks about $1^1/_2$ inches square. Add the turkey chunks to the pot and stir. Then add the rest of the water, bring to a light simmer, reduce heat to very low, and simmer without a cover until the turkey is almost done. If it's a very tough bird, you might want to consider adding a cover so that all the water won't steam off. Add more water if necessary. After about 1 hour, add the shrimp and increase the heat until the gumbo starts to bubble lightly. Reduce the heat to low, and simmer for 25 minutes. Add a little more salt and pepper if needed. Serve hot in large soup bowls and add a dollop of cooked rice in the center. Eat with hot New Orleans French bread. I like garlic butter smeared on top of the bread.

Wild Turkey Filé Gumbo

This old-timey recipe depends on a good roux and on filé. The recipe calls for lard (hog fat), but an acceptable roux can also be made from Crisco or even margarine. The filé, a thickening agent that is available in some spice selections at supermarkets and other outlets, is nothing more than powdered sassafras leaves. Since sassafras trees grow on my property, I dry my own leaves and grind them into fine powder, but the store-bought filé is suitable. The recipe also calls for a pint of oysters with liquid. These are best when they are shucked and dropped into a pint container, along with a little juice from the oyster shell. Most oysters sold in containers have been washed to remove any bits of shell or trash. This washing takes away some of the flavor, and the process wastes the wonderful salty liquid that is in the oyster's shell. This is one of my favorite recipes, and I am guilty of cooking it also with a whole chicken instead of part of a turkey. One day I'm going to try it with guinea hen or maybe a tough old cock pheasant.

> 1 wild turkey, with breast removed
> 1 pint oysters with some liquid
> ½ cup lard
> 1 cup all-purpose flour
> 2 tablespoons filé powder
> 2 medium to large onions
> 3 stalks celery with green tops
> 3 cloves garlic
> 2 tablespoons chopped fresh parsley
> salt and pepper to taste (but see note below)
> rice (cooked separately)

Melt the lard in a heavy-duty pot or stove-top Dutch oven. Stir in the flour and cook on very low heat for a long time, stirring constantly, until you have a dark brown roux. An hour isn't too long, if you have the time and the arm for such stirring. But don't burn the roux. Most experts on roux will tell you that a cast-iron pot and a wooden stirring spoon are ideal. When your roux is ready, add the chopped onions, celery, parsley, and garlic. Sauté the vegetables for a few minutes while you separate the turkey into drumsticks, thighs, and backbone. Put the drumsticks and thighs into the pot and add enough water to almost cover them. Increase the heat. Cut up the rest of the carcass as best you can to fit it into the pot. (It's not necessary to cover the bony back pieces with water.) Bring to a boil, cover tightly, reduce heat, and simmer for 40 minutes, or until the meat is tender and pulls off the bones easily. Take the meat out, bone it, and cut it into 1-inch chunks. I do this one piece at a time, working on a hand-held cutting board. After all the turkey pieces have been boned, chop the meat into bite-size chunks and return it to the pot. Pour in the oysters and the juice from the container. Bring to a boil, turn off the heat, and let the gumbo coast for 10 minutes.

At this point, you can add up to 2 tablespoons of filé powder, but be warned that the mixture should not under any circumstances be brought to another boil. Too much filé at too high a temperature will turn your gumbo into a sticky mess. The best bet, I think, is to ladle servings into individual bowls, then sprinkle on and stir in a little filé powder to taste, along with some salt and pepper.

The rice is added to the bowl of gumbo rather than the usual procedure of adding the gumbo to the rice. Serve with hot French bread.

If you plan to freeze part of the gumbo, don't add rice and filé powder to the whole batch. When you are ready to serve, thaw out the gumbo, heat it, and ladle it into bowls. Then thicken with filé and add the rice. Good stuff—and the frozen leftovers may be better than the original.

Note: Some purists won't allow black pepper in a gumbo, but personally I don't think that a little freshly ground pepper will hurt a thing. Suit yourself.

Old Tom Crockpot Gumbo

This recipe can be cooked with 2 tough cock pheasants as well as with a tom turkey. The measures below are based pretty much on what will fit into a medium-size crockpot. Usually, the thighs and drumsticks of a large old turkey will be about right. The breast can be used to cook another batch or for another recipe. Save the frame for making soup and stock for another recipe. Note that putting all the backbone into the pot will take up too much room. If you want to use it, boil it in a separate container until you can pull the meat from the bones, then put the meat into the crockpot along with the other ingredients.

> 4 pounds turkey pieces, skinned
> 1 pound cured ham, cut into 1-inch squares
> 1 medium onion, diced
> 2 cloves garlic, minced
> 2 stalks celery, chopped
> 1 large bell pepper, chopped
> 2 cups okra, cut into $1/2$-inch segments
> 2 bay leaves
> 2 tablespoons chopped parsley
> 1 tablespoon Worcestershire sauce
> 1 tablespoon chives
> 1 cup chicken or turkey stock or broth
> $1/2$ teaspoon thyme
> 1 teaspoon salt
> $1/2$ teaspoon Tabasco sauce (or more, to taste)
> mushrooms (optional)
> rice (cooked separately)

Skin the turkey pieces and put them into the crockpot. Add the ham, onion, garlic, okra, celery, bell pepper, bay leaves, parsley, chives, thyme, Worcestershire sauce, salt, and Tabasco sauce. Add the chicken stock, using it to wash down some of the spices. Add the mushrooms last, filling the crockpot to the top if you've got enough mushrooms on hand. Turn the heat to low and cook for 10 hours. An hour before eating, adjust the seasonings to taste. Remove the turkey pieces and pull the meat from the bone. Chop the meat into serving-size pieces and return it to the crockpot. Ladle the gumbo into individual serving bowls along with cooked rice.

Wild Turkey and Wheat Berry Porridge

In the Anatolia region of modern Turkey, this dish is served at festivals celebrating the wheat harvest. The recipe, a combination of lamb or poultry cooked with wheat berries, predates biblical times. Back then, large bustards and other birds of the rolling steppe were probably more widely available than chickens and were hunted with the aid of falcons. In any case, it's a great recipe for wild turkey. According to *A Turkish Cookbook*, lamb or sheep neck can also be used. I have also cooked it with neck of white-tailed deer.

> $^1/_2$ wild turkey (see below)
> $^3/_4$ pound hard wheat berries
> 2 large onions, chopped
> 2 tablespoons butter or cooking oil
> 1 teaspoon red pepper flakes
> 1 bay leaf
> salt
> water

You'll need about 3 pounds (exact measures aren't critical) of bone-in turkey; often half a wild turkey will be about right. To get some breast meat, cut the bird in half lengthwise. You can also breast the bird for use in other recipes and use what's left for this recipe. The giblets can also be added if you like.

Soak the wheat berries overnight in water. When you are ready to cook, cut the turkey into pieces and put them into a suitable pot. Cover with water and add a bay leaf. Bring to a boil, then reduce heat, cover, and simmer for an hour or two, or until the meat is very tender. Remove the bird and let it cool. (Save the stock liquid in the pot.) Pull the meat off the bones and chop it into small pieces. I use a chef's knife, but any sort of chopper will do. Fish the bay leaf out of the stock left in the pot, then add the chopped meat and pepper flakes to the liquid. Drain the wheat berries, add them to the pot, and simmer. Melt the butter or heat the oil in a frying pan and sauté the chopped onions for a few minutes. Stir in some salt, then add this mixture to the turkey and wheat. Simmer for about 30 minutes, stirring from time to time with a wooden spoon, or until you have a smooth, thick porridge.

Note: If you don't have any wheat berries, you can substitute other good whole-grain groats, such as barley or rye.

Turkey and Walnut Stew

The Europeans and Middle Easterners, as well as the American Indians, made excellent use of nuts as a thickener. The recipe below calls for English walnuts, but feel free to experiment if you have access to other nuts. The wild American black walnut, however, is a little too strong, but on the other hand, hickory nuts will do nicely.

> 1 breast of wild turkey
> 1 medium onion, minced
> 1/4 cup butter
> 3 cups chicken or turkey stock (or water with
>   bouillon cubes)
> 2 cups English walnuts
> juice of 3 lemons
> salt and pepper to taste
> 1/4 teaspoon cinnamon

Grind the walnuts in a meat grinder or mortar and pestle. Cut the turkey breast into bite-size chunks. Sprinkle these with salt and pepper. Heat the butter in a skillet, and sauté the turkey pieces on both sides until lightly browned, then drain. Sauté the chopped onion for 3 or 4 minutes, then stir in the ground walnuts. Add the chicken or turkey stock, lemon juice, cinnamon, and a little salt and pepper. Bring the mixture to a boil, stirring as you go. Reduce the heat, simmer, and stir for 10 minutes. Add the turkey pieces to the skillet contents, cover, and simmer on very low heat for 40 minutes, stirring from time to time. Serve hot over fluffy rice.

Turkey with Drop Dumplings

Some people make dumplings by first rolling the dough out to a thickness of about ⅛ inch, and then cutting it into ½-inch strips before adding them to a pot. Although these are very good, I usually prefer to make drop dumplings, unless I want to make a meat pie with a crisscrossed crust on top and dumplings mixed in with the filling. Further, I much prefer dumplings made with flour rather than cornmeal. But remember that this dish can be made with either.

Turkey
small wild turkey
1 teaspoon salt
½ teaspoon red pepper flakes
2 bay leaves
water

Cut the bird into pieces, being sure to cut the breast in half and separate the leg quarters into drumstick and thigh. Put the bony pieces in with the rest, along with the liver, gizzard, and heart. Also use the head, if you've got it. As the Florida crackers know, a turkey head has got some good gnawing on it, and the brains are simply wonderful.

Put the turkey pieces into a pot and cover it slightly with water. Add the bay leaves, salt, and red pepper. Bring to a boil, reduce heat, cover, and simmer for 2 or 3 hours, depending on how tough the meat is. If you use a jake or young hen for this recipe, it may be tender in an hour or so. In any case, it's best not to cook the meat off the bone. When the turkey is tender, drop in some dumplings, made as follows.

Dumplings
1½ cups all-purpose flour
½ cup milk
1 egg
2 teaspoons baking powder
½ teaspoon salt

Mix the flour, baking powder, and salt in a bowl. Whisk together the egg and milk. Make a hole in the flour mixture and pour in the milk and egg. Stir or beat until you have a good dough. Pull off pieces of the dough and drop them, with the aid of a spoon, into the turkey pot. Make sure that all the dumplings get into the liquid and do not sit atop the turkey pieces. Cover and simmer for 15 minutes. You can thicken the gravy, if desired, by adding a little cornstarch or flour that has been mixed into water.

This recipe usually serves 4 to 6. If I have leftovers, I like to warm up the pot, bone the meat, and add some chopped hard-boiled egg, along with a good sprinkling of freshly ground pepper. In fact, the leftovers are even better than the original. Even leftover gravy (without meat) is worth saving. It is very good over toast, biscuit halves, rice, or mashed potatoes.

Note: I prefer my dumplings small, and I use a teaspoon for dropping them into the pot. Others want a larger, more gooey dumpling and use a tablespoon. Suit yourself. Also see the other dumpling recipes in this chapter.

Cornmeal Dumplings

There are probably thousands of recipes for cornmeal dumplings, some of which call for a combination of meal and flour. Unfortunately, a good deal depends on the kind of cornmeal you are using. The following recipe, for example, works with fine, stone-ground meal, whereas the same dumplings made with most commercial yellow meals won't hold together.

In any case, here's my favorite recipe, made with Adam's stone-ground meal. Cook it with other meals at your own risk.

> 2 cups fine-ground white cornmeal
> hot broth from the turkey pot (about 2 cups)
> 1 teaspoon salt
> ½ teaspoon black pepper

Sift the cornmeal if it has weevils in it. Put it into a mixing bowl, and add 1¾ cup of the hot broth dipped from the pot in which the turkey boils. Stir in the salt and pepper. Let the mixture set for about 10 minutes. Then dip out another ¼ cup of broth and very slowly add it to the mixture, stirring as you go. Hold off on the broth if the mixture starts to get too soupy, or add a little more if needed. When you get the texture right, divide the mixture into 4 parts and roll each into a log about 1 inch in diameter. Cut each log into 1-inch segments. When the turkey is tender, drop the dumplings gently into the pot and simmer (but do not boil) for another 30 minutes. Be careful not to break up the dumplings when serving.

Wild Turkey and Easy Dumplings

Don't let the short list of ingredients in this recipe fool you. It makes a delicious hot meal for a cold winter day. Instead of rolling out dough and making dumplings from scratch, I usually buy some refrigerated flour tortillas at the grocery store, cut them into strips, and drop them into the pot toward the end of the cooking. I have also used cornmeal tortillas to advantage. But if you've got a good dumpling recipe, by all means use it.

> turkey legs and bony parts
> prepared tortillas, cut into strips
> 1 medium onion, chopped
> 1 stalk celery, chopped
> 2 hard-boiled chicken eggs, sliced
> 2 bay leaves
> salt and pepper
> water

Put the turkey legs and bony parts into a large Dutch oven or other suitable pot. Partly cover with water. Add bay leaves, salt, and pepper. Bring to a boil, cover, reduce heat, and simmer for an hour, or until the turkey is done and the meat can be pulled off the bones easily with a fork. Bone all the meat and put it back into the pot, along with the chopped celery and onion. Discard the bones and bay leaves, and add more water if needed. Bring to a new boil, cover, reduce heat, and simmer for 10 minutes. Add the tortilla strips, bring to a new boil, cover, reduce heat, and simmer for 10 minutes.

The exact measures for this recipe are not critical, but I prefer not to have too many dumplings. The liquid should be on the thick side, and the dumplings will thicken it somewhat. If it is too thin, stir in a little paste made with flour and water. If too thick, add some plain water. When the dumplings are done, carefully stir in some slices of hard-boiled eggs. Add salt and pepper to taste. I like to spoon the turkey and dumplings directly onto plates, along with some vegetables and a hot biscuit or two. The biscuits are good for sopping the gravy and cleaning up the plate after the turkey and dumplings have been eaten.

Backcountry Turkey

Here's a recipe that can be cooked with a whole turkey cut into pieces or with half a turkey. If you've got a large, tough tom to cook in camp, then consider this recipe carefully, as it is easy and requires very few ingredients, yet is very good and satisfying. The red pepper adds to the flavor, but a little goes a long way for most people.

> turkey
> water
> salt
> red pepper flakes
> cornmeal dumplings (recipe above)
> hard-boiled chicken eggs (optional)

Cut the turkey into pieces. Put it into a pot of suitable size and cover with water. Add salt and red pepper flakes. Bring to a boil, reduce heat, cover, and simmer for an hour, or until the bird is tender. Reduce heat and add cornmeal or other dumplings. Boil a couple of chicken eggs, if you've got them, slice, and add to the pot, stirring gently. Serve in bowls like soup.

Stewed Wild Turkey

Here's a dish that's easy to prepare. It can be made from legs and thighs, but I like it with the breast of a young turkey. For this recipe, use about 2 pounds of meat. The gravy is wonderful and can be served on rice, mashed potatoes, or, better, fluffy biscuit halves.

small wild turkey breast or other parts (about 2 pounds)
1 can condensed mushroom soup (10½-ounce size)
1 soup can of water
1 medium to small onion, diced
½ stalk celery, diced
1 tablespoon butter or margarine
salt and pepper

Bone the turkey breast and cut it into serving-size chunks. Mix the soup, butter, and water in a pot of suitable size. Bring to a boil, and add the onion, celery, salt, pepper, and turkey chunks. Reduce heat, cover, and simmer 1½ hours, or until tender. (Older birds may take much longer.) When the turkey is tender to the fork, taste the gravy and add a little more salt and pepper if desired. I like lots of freshly ground pepper on mine. Serve hot.

If you have leftovers, dice the meat and mix it into the gravy, and save for lunch. Heat the mixture and stir in a chopped hard boiled egg and a little cream. Serve over toast.

Helen's Favorite

My wife loves a hot, thick soup made primarily with turkey, ham bone, rice, and tomatoes. I usually make it with the turkey frame that is left after I fillet out the breast and disjoint the legs. Of course, I leave some meat on the frame. The ham part comes from either a bone (with a little meat) from a baked ham or a smoked ham hock or two purchased at the supermarket.

turkey frame
ham bone
1 can tomatoes (16-ounce size)
1 medium onion, diced
1 cup rice
$^1\!/_2$ teaspoon red pepper flakes
salt to taste
1 bay leaf
water

Put the turkey frame and the ham bone into a pot and add 4 cups of water, chopped onion, bay leaf, salt, and pepper. Bring to a boil, reduce heat, cover tightly, and simmer for $1^1\!/_2$ hours, or until the meat is very tender and almost falls off the bones. Remove the bones and discard the bay leaves. Measure the broth, making sure that you have 4 cups. (If your lid didn't fit on the pot, some of the liquid may have steamed off.) Put the liquid back into the pot, adding more water if necessary. Pull the meat off the bones, chop it, and add it to the pot. Add the tomatoes, along with the juice from the can, and cut into quarters. Bring to a boil, add the rice, bring to a new boil, reduce heat, cover, and simmer for 25 minutes. Serve in bowls with plenty of hot bread on the side. If you don't have bread, saltine crackers will do.

Crockpot Turkey

Wise cooks know that crockpots can work wonders on lean, dry meat. Even a tough old tom becomes toothsome after simmering all day in a crockpot. I usually don't follow a rigid recipe, but I normally use a can of cream soup and a few mushrooms if I can fit them in.

wild turkey
1 can condensed cream of celery soup (10$^1\!/_2$-ounce size)
8 ounces fresh mushrooms
2 bay leaves
juice of one lemon
salt and pepper to taste

Cut the bird into pieces. Rub each piece with lemon juice and fit into the crockpot as best you can. If you're still using a small crockpot that won't hold a whole turkey, you can save some for another recipe or cook it the next day. Fill the crockpot almost to the top with turkey pieces, then pile on some mushrooms and add the bay leaves. Sprinkle on some salt and pepper, then pour the soup over the top. Cover tightly, turn the heat to low, and cook for 9 or 10 hours.

The turkey will be very tender and moist, and the gravy in the bottom will go nicely with the meat and mashed potatoes, rice, or biscuit halves.

SEVEN

Ground Turkey

Ground turkey can be made into hamburgers or patties, or browned and used in casseroles or classic recipes such as spaghetti and chili. It can also be used in egg rolls and dishes like Greek moussaka. I haven't tried ground turkey in all the thousands of recipes that call for ground meat (usually beef), but I have tested quite a few, and I can report that turkey may be better than beef for most purposes. It certainly is believed to be better for your health.

It's best to chill the turkey meat or, better, partly freeze it before running it through your food processor. I like to use the old fashion hand-crank grinder with a medium blade. I recommend the following recipes for ground turkey.

Turkey Burgers

I like to cook these burgers in ¼-pound size, then put them into large hamburger buns with lettuce, tomato slices, onion, mayonnaise, catsup, and other condiments. Often I'll cook some french-fried potatoes or onion rings to go with them, but sometimes I'll settle for chips and kosher pickles.

> 1 pound ground turkey
> 1 tablespoon prepared mustard
> 1 tablespoon white-wine Worcestershire sauce
> salt and pepper to taste
> cooking oil
> hamburger buns
> condiments as desired

Mix the mustard, Worcestershire sauce, salt, and pepper with the turkey, and form four patties. Heat a little cooking oil in a skillet, and cook on medium high heat for about 4 minutes on each side, or until done. Turn carefully with a thin spatula. If the patties tend to tear apart, use two spatulas. Serve on buns with condiments.

Wild Turkey Spaghetti

Almost everybody likes spaghetti, and this is an excellent dish for introducing wild turkey to people who think they won't care for it, or for diet-conscious people who don't want the fat and cholesterol from pork or beef.

> 2 pounds ground turkey
> 2 cans tomatoes, chopped (16-ounce size)
> 2 stalks celery with green tops, chopped
> 8 ounces fresh mushrooms, sliced
> 1 large onion, chopped
> 5 cloves garlic, minced
> 1 can tomato paste (6-ounce size)
> 1 large green bell pepper, diced
> 1 tablespoon chopped fresh parsley
> $^{1}/_{2}$ tablespoon oregano
> 2 tablespoons vegetable oil
> salt and black pepper to taste
> 3 bay leaves
> 16-ounce package of spaghetti (cooked separately)
> grated Parmesan cheese (optional)

Heat the vegetable oil in a skillet or wok. Brown the turkey lightly, then stir in the onion, garlic, celery and tops, mushrooms, parsley, bay leaves, oregano, and bell pepper. Sauté for 5 minutes. Stir in the tomato paste and the tomatoes, along with the juice. Add salt and pepper. Simmer for 10 minutes, taste, and adjust the seasonings if desired. Remove the bay leaves. Meanwhile, cook the spaghetti. Follow the directions on the spaghetti package. Serve the turkey sauce over the cooked spaghetti, along with, of course, plenty of colorful salad, Italian bread, and vino. I like some grated Parmesan cheese on my spaghetti, and I really prefer it freshly grated.

This recipe will serve 6 or 8 people nicely. If you don't need that much, cut the measures in half.

Turkey Patties

This wonderful recipe calls for fish sauce, a standard ingredient in much of Southeast Asia. It can be found in food shops that specialize in oriental ingredients and even in some American supermarkets, or purchased by mail order. Essentially, the fish sauce is made by packing well-salted small fish in wooden barrels. The liquid that drips out is fish sauce. The ancient Roman epicures also enjoyed a similar fish sauce made in the same manner.

> 1 pound ground turkey
> 8 chicken eggs, beaten
> 4 green onions with about half the green tops, minced
> 4 tablespoons fish sauce
> 2 tablespoons flour
> $^{1}/_{3}$ teaspoon black pepper
> cooking oil

Beat the eggs lightly and stir them into the ground turkey. Stir in the fish sauce, chopped onion, and black pepper. Sprinkle some of the flour lightly on top and stir it in, being careful to avoid lumping; repeat until all the flour has been added. Heat a little oil in a small skillet (9-inch) or on a griddle. Spoon part of the mixture into the hot skillet, as when making pancakes. Cook until the bottom of the patty browns nicely, then turn with a spatula and cook the other side. Remove and cook the rest of the mix in the same manner.

Serve hot, along with the bottle of fish sauce for anyone who wants to sprinkle on a little more.

Old Tom Breakfast Sausage Patties

If you've got an old bird that is too tough to chew, grind it up and make this breakfast sausage. The measures below are for 1 pound of meat. Weigh your ground turkey and adjust the other ingredients accordingly, or freeze the ground turkey in convenient 1-pound packages and whip up a fresh batch whenever you want it.

  1 pound ground turkey
  1 chicken egg, beaten
  ¼ teaspoon dried sage
  ½ teaspoon dried thyme
  1 teaspoon black pepper
  salt to taste
  cooking oil

Mix everything but the oil in a bowl and refrigerate. When you are ready to cook, shape the mixture into patties ½ inch thick. Heat a little oil in a skillet or on a griddle. Sauté the patties for a few minutes on each side, until nicely browned and cooked through. These are good for breakfast, served with toast and eggs or pancakes. They also make a tasty sandwich, along with a fried egg and mayonnaise.

Italian Turkey Sausage Patties

Ground turkey makes an excellent Italian sausage, which is distinguished by the flavor of fennel seeds and garlic.

  2 pounds ground turkey
  1 tablespoon olive oil
  4 cloves garlic, minced
  2 teaspoons crushed fennel seeds
  salt and black pepper to taste

Grind the turkey, using either dark or light meat or both. Mix in the other ingredients and refrigerate for several hours. When you are ready to cook, shape the sausage meat into patties and fry in a little oil on a griddle until done.

Turkey Goulash

Except for the Hungarian variety, usually made with red meat and plenty of mild paprika, I'll put goulash in the same boat with the casserole—usually good and easy to prepare, but not memorable. Here's one to try.

> 1 pound ground turkey
> 1 medium onion, chopped
> 1 clove garlic, minced
> 1 can tomato paste (6-ounce size)
> 3 cans water (6-ounce size)
> 1/4 cup grated Parmesan cheese
> 1 teaspoon dried basil
> salt and pepper to taste
> 8 ounces macaroni, cooked separately
> 1 tablespoon oil or margarine

Heat the oil in a skillet, and lightly brown the ground turkey and onion. Stir in the tomato paste. Slosh some water around in the tomato paste can and pour it into the skillet. Add two more cans of water. Stir in the garlic, basil, salt, and pepper. Reduce heat, cover, and simmer for 25 minutes. Meanwhile, cook the macaroni according the directions on the package. When the skillet dish has simmered for 25 minutes, stir in the macaroni. Sprinkle with freshly grated Parmesan. Serve hot.

Wild Turkey Sausage Links

If you've got a smoker, or a silo-shaped cooker-smoker with water pan and chip box, be sure to try this recipe. You'll need some casings, which are sold by some mail-order houses. Casings may also be available through your local meat processor or sausage maker.

6 pounds boneless turkey
casings
$1/2$ cup bacon drippings
2 ounces of Morton's Quick Cure salt or sea salt
2 tablespoons black pepper
2 tablespoons brown sugar
3 cloves, ground
8 allspice berries, ground

I like to grind my own peppercorns and sea salt for this recipe, along with the cloves and allspice. Freshly ground spices and seasonings taste better and smell better, and sea salt has more minerals than regular table salt. I use a small mortar and pestle, finding it faster and better than most pepper mills. If you aren't inclined to grind everything, substitute ground black pepper and Morton's Quick Cure salt, which can be purchased in most supermarkets, along with a little ground cloves and allspice.

Bone the turkey and grind the meat in a meat grinder with a $3/16$-inch plate. (Both boning and grinding will be easier if you first chill the meat.) Spread the meat out on the counter, and sprinkle it all over with the seasonings, bacon drippings, and salt cure. Then grind all the meat again.

Wash and stuff the casings, twisting every 8 or 10 inches, or in links of a convenient size. Don't cut the sausage at this time. Put the stuffed sausage in cool place for 24 hours, allowing the cure to work. Then smoke it by one means or another, depending on your experience and your smoking equipment. An ordinary silo smoker with an electric heat element (variable), wood chip box, and water pan will do a good job. Merely coil the sausage around on the top rack, and smoke for 3 or 4 hours at 150 degrees. Then increase the heat to 160 degrees for several more hours. The internal temperature of the sausage should reach 155 degrees, so that it will be fully cooked. You can also cold-smoke the sausage for a day or so, then cook it fully before eating. In either case, the cured sausage can be stored for several days in the refrigerator or frozen longer for storage.

Wild Turkey Chili

I'll make no secret of the fact that venison is my favorite meat for making chili, simply because it holds up well under long cooking. But I can stir up a good mess of chili with ground turkey, and you can too. Here's all you'll need:

> 2 pounds ground turkey
> 1 can tomato paste (6-ounce size)
> 2 cans water (6-ounce size)
> 2 tablespoons cooking oil
> 1 teaspoon red pepper flakes
> 2 teaspoons crushed cumin seeds
> 1 teaspoon salt
> rice or pinto beans, cooked separately (optional)
> chilled chopped onions (optional)
> sour cream (optional)

Heat the oil and sauté the ground turkey for about 5 minutes, or until lightly browned. Stir in the tomato paste, water, red pepper, salt, and cumin. Cover and simmer (do not boil) for 30 minutes. Serve in a bowl. Add your choice of mix-ins or toppings, such as pinto beans, rice, chopped onions, or sour cream. Sometimes I like to mix in some rice and chopped canned tomatoes, then eat the result with saltines.

Variations: Try ground turkey in any chili recipe calling for ground beef. You also can mix the meats half and half if you like.

Turkey Balls

Here's a tasty ground turkey dish that is easy to prepare. It can be made with any part of the turkey, but I prefer a mixture of breast and thigh or leg. It can be made from a tough old tom or a young bird.

2 pounds ground turkey
all-purpose flour
2 chicken eggs, lightly beaten
2 tablespoons white-wine Worcestershire sauce
4 cloves garlic, minced
2 tablespoons finely chopped fresh chives or onion tops
salt and pepper to taste
peanut oil

Chill the turkey meat and grind it with a medium grate. Mix turkey, eggs, garlic, chives or onion tops, 2 tablespoons flour, white-wine Worcestershire sauce, salt, and pepper. Shape the mixture into balls about 1 inch in diameter. Heat some peanut oil to 375 degrees in a deep fryer. When the oil is ready, roll the turkey balls in flour and fry in the hot oil until they are golden brown; this will take only 4 or 5 minutes. Do not overcook. Drain on a brown bag. Serve as appetizers or as a main course. I like them with a thick pepper sauce, such as Pickapepper.

EIGHT

Sandwiches and Loaves

My wife cooks wonderful biscuits, but she doesn't make a sandwich quite the way I want it. She usually gets the two pieces of bread back together in a symmetrical way, but something is always missing: meat and mayonnaise. She shorts me on the meat and mayonnaise. I really don't think that I am all that fussy, and I wouldn't have brought up this point if I were doing a book on beef or pork. But this is a book on cooking turkey, and I insist on having plenty of mayonnaise on the sandwiches. Of course, the best mayonnaise is homemade. Store-bought mayonnaise of good quality will do, but avoid the cheap stuff.

Cold Turkey Sandwich

I wrote some time ago about what I consider to be the best of all sandwiches, and one of the best ways to eat turkey, in my book *Good Vittles*. Since I haven't changed my mind, I see no need to rewrite the text. Here's all you'll need:

> cold turkey
> white bread
> homemade mayonnaise
> freshly ground black pepper

"Chill the turkey and the mayonnaise. Get some good white bread, soft, very soft, and slice it a little thick. . . . If you don't make your own bread, try the regular white bread from the grocery store or bakery, but not the thin sandwich slices. Get two pieces of bread and spread each slice generously with the mayonnaise.

"Slice the turkey thin. Cut some slices with the grain and some against the grain, giving a variety in texture. I use a fillet knife for this purpose, but any good knife will do. Pile the turkey high onto one piece of bread, using six or seven slices, then sprinkle with pepper to taste. Top with the other piece of bread. Use no lettuce, no pickles, or other such stuff. Just make sure that you've got very soft bread with plenty of mayonnaise on it.

"Cut the sandwich in half, diagonally. Go ahead. Take the first bite right out of the middle."

Turkey Buns

I usually make this dish with chopped meat from boiled legs and thighs, but it can be made from breast meat or a combination of light and dark. You can also use leftover turkey for this purpose. Coarsely ground meat will work, but I normally use a chef's knife to dice the meat into small pieces because it's easier to wash a knife than a food processor or meat grinder. As a rule, I buy a package of shredded cheddar cheese, then reduce it to smaller pieces with the chef's knife.

2 cups diced turkey
1 cup cheddar cheese, finely shredded or diced
$1/2$ cup green pepper, finely chopped
$1/2$ cup onion, finely chopped
salt and pepper to taste
8 hamburger buns
sauce of your choice (optional)

Preheat the oven to 375 degrees. Mix turkey, cheese, green pepper, onion, salt, and pepper. Open the buns and spoon equal amounts of the turkey mixture onto each bottom half. Top with the other bun half, and wrap each sandwich in aluminum foil. Put into the center of the oven and bake for 15 minutes. Eat hot, along with potato chips or potato salad. I like to open my burger and spread on a little sauce. Ordinary ketchup does nicely, but I prefer a thick pepper sauce, such as Pickapepper or Dat'l Do-it.

Sloppy Joes with Turkey

I don't know where the name "sloppy joe" came from, but it refers to an open-faced sandwich topped with ground meat in a thick sauce. Kids love it, possibly because the name gives them license to make a mess at the table. Typically, hamburger buns and ground beef are used. But ground venison, turkey, and other good meats are just as good and sometimes better. This recipe calls for diced leftover turkey, but ground raw turkey can also be browned in a skillet and used to advantage.

> 2 cups diced leftover turkey
> 2 strips bacon
> 1 medium onion, diced
> 2 cloves garlic, minced
> 1/2 cup catsup
> 1 tablespoon white-wine Worcestershire sauce
> 1 tablespoon prepared mustard
> 1 teaspoon prepared horseradish
> salt and pepper to taste
> 4 hamburger buns

In a skillet, cook the bacon until crisp, put it on absorbent paper to drain, and sauté the chopped onion and garlic in the bacon drippings. Pour off the excess pan grease, then mix in the catsup, white-wine Worcestershire, mustard, horseradish, salt, and pepper. Stir in crumbled bacon, and simmer for about 10 minutes to blend the flavors. Then stir in the turkey and simmer for another 10 minutes or so. Toast the inside faces of 4 hamburger buns. Put both halves of a bun, toasted side up, on a plate and top with meat sauce. Serve with thick potato chips or french fries and large dill pickles. Coleslaw rounds out the meal—if you can get the kids to eat it.

Variations: To use ground fresh turkey instead of leftovers, fry the bacon as usual, then sauté the meat and chopped onions for about 10 minutes in the bacon drippings. Then add the sauce ingredients, stir, and simmer for 10 minutes.

Grilled Turkey Sandwiches

This sandwich is an excellent way to use leftover turkey. I "grill" the sandwiches in a skillet or on a griddle, or broil them in the oven about 3 inches from the heating coil. Small countertop ovens or broilers work nicely for a couple of sandwiches. The measures below will make a filling for 8 sandwiches. The spread can be refrigerated for a couple of days, but I do not recommend freezing it. If you want a smaller amount, reduce the measures accordingly.

> 2 cups chopped cooked turkey
> $\frac{1}{2}$ cup finely chopped celery
> $\frac{1}{2}$ cup mayonnaise
> salt and pepper to taste
> soft margarine spread
> American cheese slices
> sliced bread

Mix chicken, celery, mayonnaise, salt, and pepper. Heat a griddle or skillet, or preheat the broiler. Spread sandwich mix onto a slice of bread, and top with a slice of cheese and another piece of bread. Spread both slices of bread with margarine. Broil or grill until browned on both sides. Serve hot.

Turkey Cranberry Sandwich

I like to make this sandwich with leftover roast turkey and leftover cranberry sauce. The cranberry sauce recipe in chapter 10 spreads nicely. If you use the canned cranberry sauce, slice it thinly and spread it the best you can.

> thinly sliced cooked turkey
> fresh sandwich bread
> mayonnaise
> Dijon or Creole mustard
> lettuce
> cranberry sauce

Spread both sides of the bread lightly with the mayonnaise and mustard. Arrange the turkey slices on one side. Spread on the cranberry sauce, then top with a crisp lettuce leaf and the other piece of bread.

Club Sandwich

In my opinion, a club sandwich is made with three pieces of white bread with the crust trimmed off. Other books, however, may offer different specifications and even different ingredients.

> thinly sliced cooked turkey breast
> white bread
> crisp bacon
> lettuce
> sliced tomato
> mayonnaise
> salt and pepper
> stuffed olives (optional)

Use three large slices of fresh white bread for each sandwich. Trim off the crust. Spread the first slice with mayonnaise, then put down a lettuce leaf and a slice or two of tomato. Break three pieces of bacon in half and arrange on the lettuce. Top with a little mayonnaise, salt, and pepper. Place the second piece of bread on top, and spread lightly with mayonnaise. Top with turkey slices, salt, pepper, and mayonnaise. Top with the third slice of bread. Cut the sandwich diagonally into 4 triangular pieces. Put a stuffed olive on each piece and pin with a toothpick.

Easy Sandwich Spread

If you enjoy a crunchy sandwich spread, as I do, be sure to try this recipe whenever you have leftover turkey. It will keep for a couple of days in the refrigerator, but I don't recommend freezing any spread that contains mayonnaise.

2 cups chopped cooked turkey
$1/2$ cup chopped cashew nuts
6 tablespoons mayonnaise
4 tablespoons chopped salad pickles
juice from one small lemon
bread or hamburger buns

Mix the first five ingredients and refrigerate. To serve, spread on sandwich bread or hamburger buns.

Easy Turkey Loaf

Although this recipe can be made with leftovers, I like to make it with part of the meat left after boiling a breasted turkey. It's best to chill the meat, then grind it with the coarse blade of a sausage mill. The recipe also calls for giblet gravy and a cup of turkey stock. If you don't have turkey stock on hand, use 1 cup water and a chicken bouillon cube. The giblets from the turkey can be used for the gravy. These can also be frozen with part of the stock if you want to make the gravy later.

4 cups ground cooked turkey
1 cup turkey stock
1 cup milk
2 chicken eggs, beaten
2 cups soft bread crumbs
1 small onion (golf-ball size), chopped
1 teaspoon salt
$1/2$ teaspoon black pepper
giblet gravy (see recipe in chapter 10)

Preheat the oven to 375 degrees and grease a loaf pan. Mix all the ingredients, and pour into the loaf pan. Bake for an hour. Slice the loaf and serve hot with giblet gravy.

You can also slice this loaf and use it for hot or cold sandwich meat.

NINE

Leftovers and Surprises

If I have done a good job in writing this book and if both the hunter and the cook exercise reasonable care in handling and cooking the wild turkey, there shouldn't be many leftovers. Yet, if you serve up this festive bird as part of a big spread on some special occasion, leftovers of one sort or another are inevitable. The recipes below show that leftovers (or boiled turkey) don't have to be dull fare.

Turkey Scrapple

If you like scrapple for breakfast, be sure to try this recipe the next time you have leftover roast turkey, dressing, and giblet gravy. Turkey scrapple will keep nicely in the refrigerator for a few days, and it can be frozen for even longer storage.

> 4 cups diced cooked turkey
> 4 cups stuffing or dressing
> 1½ cups white cornmeal
> ½ cup (or more) giblet gravy
> 1 chopped onion
> 2 teaspoons celery salt
> black pepper
> bones of wild turkey
> water

When you carve the turkey, be sure to save the bones from the drumstick, thighs, and back. Cut off most of the leftover meat, chop it, and put it aside. Crack the bones or break them, put them into a large pot, add the chopped onion, and cover with water. Bring to a boil, then reduce heat and simmer for 30 minutes. Remove the bones from the pot and measure the liquid, then add enough water to make 12 cups total. Pull the meat from the bones and chop it. Measure the meat and add enough from the pile you set aside to make 4 cups. Add the meat and 4 cups of stuffing (chopped or broken up) to the liquid in the pot. Stir in the gravy, celery salt, and pepper. Bring to heat, slowly stirring in the cornmeal, and stir until the mixture is quite thick. Pour or ladle the mixture into well-greased bread pans and chill.

To serve, slice as needed, and fry the pieces in a little oil until nicely browned. Although scrapple is traditionally eaten for break-fast, I like it at any time. Of course, the spices used in the dish can be varied to suit your taste or what you have on hand. I like to put some red pepper flakes in the water while boiling the turkey bones, then omit the black pepper. Also, sage, used sparingly, goes nicely with wild turkey scrapple.

Easy Turkey Salad

Here's a quick recipe for making a good turkey salad. I like to serve it for lunch on a lettuce leaf, along with whole-wheat crackers.

> diced left-over turkey
> apples, peeled and diced
> celery, diced
> lemon juice
> chopped pecans or other nuts
> mayonnaise

Mix everything well and chill. I have no measurements to offer for the ingredients, so you'll have to come up with your own mix. It's hard to go wrong if you go easy on the celery—and use plenty of mayonnaise.

Wild Turkey Salad

My family likes this recipe for lunch, served on green lettuce or made into sandwiches. I also like it atop crackers. Although it can be made with leftover baked turkey, I prefer steamed or boiled meat. We make it with what's left of the turkey after I have filleted the breast for stir-frying or grilling. The measures below are somewhat tentative, however, and should depend partly on how much meat is on the bird. It's really best to chop up the cooked turkey, then add enough of the other ingredients to suit your taste.

> wild turkey parts
> 4 hard-boiled chicken eggs
> 2 or 3 stalks of celery with tops, chopped
> 2 or 3 medium onions, chopped
> 1/2 red bell pepper, chopped (optional)
> chopped fresh parsley (optional)
> 1 cup finely chopped pecans
> mayonnaise or salad dressing
> 1 tablespoon chopped salad pickles
> juice from pickle jar
> 3 bay leaves
> salt and pepper to taste
> water

After cutting out the breast meat for other purposes, reduce the bird to parts that will fit into a Dutch oven or other heavy pot. Add enough water to almost cover the meat and bones. Bring to a boil, and add bay leaves, salt, and pepper. Reduce heat, cover, and simmer for 40 minutes, or until the meat is tender. Remove the meat and reserve the liquid for soup stock. When the turkey is cool, pull the meat off the bones, chop it, and put it into a large mixing bowl. Chop the eggs and add to the bowl, along with the pecans. Then finely chop and add the celery and part of the tops, red bell pepper, fresh parsley, and onion. (I recommend the red pepper and green parsley mostly for color, but they can be omitted.) Mix in some mayonnaise, chopped pickles, and a little liquid from the pickle jar. Stir well, adding a little more mayonnaise if needed to keep the salad nicely moist.

Leftovers Hash

Using up a whole turkey and the stuffing or dressing can sometimes be a problem. Here's an easy dish to make, but you will need a large skillet with an ovenproof handle. Cast iron is perfect.

> 4 cups diced leftover turkey
> 2 cups leftover dressing or stuffing
> 2 medium onions, chopped
> 1 green bell pepper, chopped
> 1 red bell pepper, chopped
> 6 chicken eggs, whisked
> 2 tablespoons cream or milk
> $\frac{1}{2}$ cup margarine
> $\frac{1}{2}$ cup pecan pieces
> 1 cup freshly grated Parmesan cheese
> $\frac{1}{4}$ cup minced fresh parsley
> salt and pepper

Preheat the oven broiler. Melt the margarine in the skillet on top of the stove. Sauté the onion, bell peppers, and parsley for a few minutes. Stir in the turkey, dressing, pecans, salt, and pepper. Heat for a few minutes. Whisk the eggs and mix in the grated Parmesan and the cream or milk. Pour into the skillet with the meat mixture, stir, and cook on low heat until the eggs set. Put the skillet under the broiler for a few minutes to brown the top of the hash. Serve directly from the skillet.

Turkey on Toast

For this recipe, I normally use what's left of the wild turkey after filleting out the breast. This includes the neck and giblets, unless you are saving them for some other recipe. The exact measure of the meat isn't too important, but don't cut back too much lest the result be too thin.

> wild turkey parts
> 5 cups water
> 1 large onion, diced
> 2 stalks of celery with tops, chopped
> ³/₄ cup flour mixed with 1 cup cold water
> 1 tablespoon chopped fresh parsley
> 2 teaspoons salt
> ¹/₂ teaspoon red pepper flakes
> 3 bay leaves

Disjoint the turkey and put the pieces into a large pot or Dutch oven of suitable size. Add 5 cups water, bay leaves, celery, parsley, onion, salt, and red pepper flakes. Bring to a boil, reduce heat, cover, and simmer for an hour, or until the turkey meat is tender. Remove the turkey pieces, drain, and pull the meat from the bones. Chop the meat into pieces and put them back into the pot. Bring to a boil. Mix the flour into a cup of water, stirring to mix well. Stir the flour paste into the turkey and bring to a new boil. Reduce heat and simmer for a few minutes. Serve for lunch on toast or biscuit halves. Leftovers can be frozen for future use.

A. D.'s Armadillo Eggs

One day my wife and I dropped into a small Mexican restaurant for lunch. They had an appetizer called "armadillo eggs," and of course I asked our waitress, who wasn't Mexican, what exactly they were. She told me only that they were very good. Partly because an armadillo or two had been scratching up the ground along my fencerow, I pushed for an answer. But my wife's frown indicated that I should let it drop. I did, however, order several to satisfy my curiosity. They were indeed good. When we finished, the manager of the joint, no doubt having heard of my questions, came over to our table and asked how we liked the armadillo eggs.

"They're great," I said. "I'm fond of armadillos, but until now

I've always thrown the eggs away." The guy didn't know quite what to say and left without giving me their recipe. I had, however, figured that it was nothing but a jalapeño pepper stuffed with cheese, coated with a batter, and deep-fried. This was all I needed to come up with the following recipe.

> 12 jalapeño peppers
> 1/2 cup cooked turkey, grated
> 1/2 cup cheddar cheese, grated
> 1/2 cup milk
> salt
> 2 medium chicken eggs
> oil for deep frying
> all purpose flour

For this recipe, I like fresh peppers if I can get them. Cut off the top and scoop out the seeds and the inner pith, which is really hot stuff. (See the caution under Mexican Stuffed Turkey in chapter 3.) This can be done with a small knife, but I use an old baby spoon. When all of the peppers have been cleaned, simmer them in water for about 20 minutes, or until they are tender. If you use canned jalapeños, proceed as directed above but omit the simmering.

Mix the grated cheese, turkey, and salt, then stuff each pepper. Lightly beat the chicken eggs with the milk. Roll each pepper in the flour, dip in the beaten egg, and roll again in flour. (The last time I cooked armadillo eggs, I had trouble getting enough flour to stick to the slick pepper skins. My wife came to the rescue by mixing a little flour into the egg, thickening things up considerably.) Rig for deep frying. When the temperature of the oil reaches 375 degrees, fry the peppers a few at a time for 1 minute or less. Remove the armadillo eggs as soon as they are brown. Drain on a brown bag and serve warm.

Variations: Any good meat can be substituted for the wild turkey in this recipe. Also try domestic pork or javelina. Or armadillo, for that matter, if you can catch one. If you don't want to make armadillo eggs, try mincing fresh jalapeño peppers (uncooked) and mixing them in with the cheese and meat. Shape into little balls about the size of marbles, roll in the egg, dust heavily with flour, and deep-fry for a minute or two, until they are nicely browned. Call these armadillo balls.

Turkey à la King

There are a number of good recipes for this dish. Most cooks make a batch in a pot or saucepan and either serve it over toast points or sprinkle pieces of toast on top. I like to serve it atop whole pieces of toast made from good white bread.

> 2 cups diced cooked turkey meat
> 2 cups milk
> 2 cups turkey or chicken broth
> ³/₄ cup margarine
> ³/₄ cup all-purpose flour
> ¹/₂ green bell pepper, diced
> ¹/₂ red bell pepper, diced
> 8 ounces fresh mushrooms, sliced
> 1 chicken egg yolk
> salt and pepper
> 2 teaspoons mild paprika

Heat the margarine in a large skillet, and sauté the diced peppers and mushrooms for a few minutes. Add the flour and stir until you have a smooth paste. Stir in the broth, milk, salt, pepper, and paprika. Whisk the egg yolk, and stir it into the mixture. Add the cubed turkey. Simmer for a few minutes, but do not boil. Serve on toast.

Note: If you don't have any broth on hand, mix 2 chicken bouillon cubes with 2 cups hot water. You can substitute canned pimento for the red bell pepper.

Wild Turkey Casserole

This recipe is ideal for using up leftover baked turkey, but you can use boiled or steamed meat. The breast meat works better, but I have also used meat taken from the thighs and legs. The topping of crushed chips gives a pleasing contrast in texture.

> 2 cups diced cooked turkey meat
> 2 stalks chopped celery, with part of green tops
> $^1/_2$ cup slivered almonds
> juice of 2 large lemons
> 1 small onion (golf-ball size), grated
> 1 cup mayonnaise
> 1 cup crushed potato chips
> $^1/_2$ cup grated or shredded cheddar cheese
> salt and pepper to taste

Preheat the oven to 400 degrees and grease a 2-quart casserole dish suitable for serving. In a bowl, mix the turkey, celery, mayonnaise, lemon juice, onion, salt, almonds, and pepper. Put this mixture into the casserole dish, and sprinkle the top with cheese and chips. Bake for 8 minutes, then check to see whether the top is golden brown. If not, bake for a couple more minutes, but be careful not to burn.

This recipe makes a nice lunch for 4 people. It can also be served as a side dish for a main meal.

Note: This is a rather bland dish. If you want to heat it up, stir in 2 or 3 chopped jalapeño peppers.

Stuffed Green Chili Peppers

Anyone who insists on having an exact identification of the hundreds of hot pepper varieties that have been developed is reading the wrong book. I gave up on this years ago. Part of the problem is that a certain pepper may be called one thing in one part of the world and something quite different in another part of the world. The peppers that I am talking about here, however, are about 4 inches long and are sometimes available in American supermarkets. I think they are grown commercially in California. The recipe can also be adapted for other green peppers, such as mild or hot banana peppers.

$^1/_2$ pound 4-inch green chili peppers
$^1/_2$ pound minced cooked turkey breast
2 green onions with half of tops, minced
1 teaspoon soy sauce
cooking oil

Cut off the tops of the peppers with a knife and carefully scoop out the seeds and pith with a small knife or baby spoon. (See the caution under Mexican Stuffed Turkey in chapter 3.) Preheat the oven to 350 degrees. Mix the turkey, green onions, soy sauce, and 1 tablespoon oil, and stuff the peppers. Grease a baking dish of suitable size with cooking oil, then fit in the stuffed peppers. Brush the peppers with additional oil. Bake in the center of the oven for about 30 minutes.

Stuffed Bell Peppers

I have always been fond of stuffed bell peppers, but many recipes are too bland to suit me. For this reason, I like to use a little hot sauce of some sort in the stuffing along with a hot cheese topping.

2 cups diced cooked turkey
1 cup cooked rice
4 medium to large green bell peppers
1 tablespoon chopped parsley
1 small onion (golf-ball size), diced
1 can tomato sauce (8-ounce size)
2 tablespoons margarine
1 tablespoon thick hot sauce (see note below)
salt to taste
cheese with jalapeño, grated

Preheat the oven to 350 degrees. Cut the tops off the green peppers and scoop out the pulp and seeds. Put the peppers into a suitable pan and boil them for about 5 minutes, then drain the peppers. Heat the margarine in a skillet, and sauté the onion and parsley for 4 or 5 minutes. Stir in the rice, turkey, tomato sauce, hot sauce, and salt.

Stuff the peppers with this mixture, then sprinkle some grated cheese on top of each. Stand the stuffed peppers in a small oven-proof dish and bake for 30 minutes. Each pepper will serve one person for lunch or for a light main dinner course. But I'll eat two if I've got them to spare.

Note: The thick hot sauce is available in several variations, such as Pickapeppa or Dat'l Do-It sauce. These are as thick as steak sauce or catsup but contain hot peppers and other ingredients. If you prefer, you can omit the hot sauce entirely, use a spicy hot tomato sauce, or add a little Worcestershire and Tabasco to the regular tomato sauce.

Nutty Casserole

This is one of my favorite casseroles, and I make it with coarsely chopped salted peanuts. Since I was raised on a peanut farm, I often roast my own peanuts in a cast-iron skillet, or fry them in hot peanut oil and then drain them on a brown bag.

> 1 cup chopped cooked turkey
> 2 hard-boiled chicken eggs, chopped
> 1 can condensed cream of chicken soup (10½-ounce size)
> ½ cup mayonnaise
> ½ cup cracker crumbs
> ½ cup chopped roasted peanuts
> 1 stalk celery, chopped
> 1 small onion (golf-ball size), minced
> 2 tablespoons white-wine Worcestershire sauce
> salt and pepper to taste

Preheat the oven to 350 degrees and grease a casserole dish. Set the peanuts aside, then mix the other ingredients and put them into the casserole dish. Sprinkle the peanuts on top. Bake uncovered in the center of the oven for 25 to 30 minutes, or until the top is nicely browned.

Avocado Stuffed with Smoked Turkey

This recipe works best with avocados that are soft and quite ripe. Those that have ripened on a tree are the very best, but most supermarket avocados will do if they are allowed to ripen enough. If they are green and hard when you buy them, plan several days ahead.

> 1 cup diced smoked turkey
> 2 large ripe avocados
> 4 hard-boiled chicken eggs
> $^1/_3$ cup olive oil
> $^1/_4$ cup milk
> 2 limes or lemons
> $^1/_2$ teaspoon salt
> $^1/_4$ teaspoon sugar
> paprika

Peel the whites off the egg yolks and set aside. Mash the yolks in a bowl with the milk. Add salt, sugar, and the juice of a large lime or lemon. Stir in the olive oil a little at a time. Stir in the smoked turkey. Chop the egg whites and add to the bowl. Refrigerate.

When you are ready to eat, cut the avocados in half, remove the pits, and fill the cavities with the turkey mixture. Sprinkle lightly with mild paprika. Serve on a lettuce leaf, along with crackers and a lemon or lime wedge.

Variation: Add some chopped mild onion or a little chopped parsley. I have seen avocado oil for sale, and one of these days I'm going to try it instead of olive oil.

Santa Fe Turkey Salad

This very good recipe is adapted from a book called *Turkey, the Magic Ingredient,* which says the following: "This piquant salad takes you to the Southwest in flavor and color. Don't stint on the fresh cilantro; it adds a delicious dimension to the taste. Serve it in lettuce cups or to stuff tomatoes. It also makes a great taco filling or tostada topping with some shredded lettuce and chopped ripe tomato."

>1½ cups cooked turkey
>⅔ cup red, yellow, or green peppers, chopped
>½ cup cooked whole-kernel corn
>2 tablespoons red onion, chopped
>¼ cup carrots, coarsely shredded
>¼ cup chopped fresh cilantro
>2 tablespoons light olive oil
>1 teaspoon lemon juice
>1 tablespoon red wine vinegar
>1 teaspoon chili powder
>¼ teaspoon dried red pepper flakes
>salt and freshly ground pepper

Cut the turkey into thin strips 1 or 2 inches long. Mix the olive oil, lemon juice, vinegar, chili powder, red pepper flakes, salt, and ground pepper. Put the meat into a bowl and pour the olive oil mixture over it, tossing to coat all sides. Add the chopped peppers, corn, onion, carrots, and cilantro. Toss well and refrigerate for an hour or two before serving.

Stuffed Tomatoes

You can peel tomatoes easily if you first immerse them in boiling water for a minute. The skin comes right off. But I must confess that I usually leave the skin on.

>1 pound finely chopped cooked turkey
>6 large tomatoes
>¼ cup finely chopped fresh parsley
>¼ cup grated cheddar cheese
>¼ cup Italian bread crumbs
>3 tablespoons melted butter or margarine
>juice of one lemon
>salt and pepper to taste

Preheat the oven to 350 degrees. Grease a baking dish that will hold the 6 tomatoes nicely. Cut the stem ends off the tomatoes and scoop out the seeds and pulp. (Save for soups, salsa, or some other use.) Sprinkle the insides with salt and pepper. Mix the turkey, parsley, lemon juice, and butter. Stuff the tomatoes with the turkey mixture. Mix the cheese and bread crumbs and sprinkle over the tops. Place the stuffed tomatoes into the baking dish and bake in the center of the oven for 20 to 25 minutes.

Wild Turkey Spread

Eating leftovers can sometimes be a problem, especially if you eat lots of them and are tired of turkey sandwiches. Here's a recipe that will help. I like it for an appetizer or for a TV snack.

> leftover cooked turkey
> Creole mustard (or Dijon)
> wine vinegar
> salt and pepper to taste

Chop the turkey finely, or, better, run it through a meat grinder with a coarse blade. Put the meat into a pan and add enough water to almost cover it. Bring to a light boil, reduce heat, and simmer for about 5 minutes. Remove the pan from the heat. Stir in a little Creole mustard and wine vinegar, along with some salt and pepper. All of the ingredients should be added to taste slowly, keeping the texture right for a spread. Refrigerate. Serve on wheat crackers or rye thins.

Helen's Latest

I'll be honest about it. I can't remember a recipe for a really good casserole, although I don't remember ever eating a bad one. I like them well enough, but they are seldom memorable. By casserole I mean a sort of one-dish meal made by layering ground meat, rice, vegetables, pasta, sauce stuff, cheese, and other such foods in an ovenproof dish and baking them in the oven. I'll also have to add that my wife is the casserole cook in our house. Whenever I want to "throw something together" for dinner, I'll reach for the skillet. She'll reach for the baking pan. We must have eaten a thousand casseroles together during our marriage, no two exactly alike. She always seems to come up with something different, and she is hard to pin down on what's in it. Here's her latest creation, made with ground turkey, which can be used in a thousand other recipes. I call it tortilla enchilada lasagna.

> 2 cups cooked turkey, ground
> 12 small corn tortillas
> 1 cup shredded Monterey Jack cheese
> 2 fresh tomatoes, chopped
> 2 cans green chilies (4-ounce size)
> 2 fresh jalapeño peppers
> 1 medium onion, chopped
> 4 cloves garlic, minced
> ¼ cup chopped cilantro
> 1 teaspoon ground cumin
> ¼ cup cooking oil
> 2 cups shredded lettuce for topping
> 1 cup sour cream for topping

Preheat the oven to 350 degrees. Carefully remove the seeds and inner pith from both the jalapeño and canned peppers. (See the caution under Mexican Stuffed Turkey in chapter 3.) In a skillet, heat the oil. Sauté the chopped onion and garlic for about 5 minutes. Stir in the cilantro, jalapeño peppers, canned peppers, chopped tomato, and cumin. Cook and stir for 5 minutes. Add the turkey, stir, and cook for another 5 minutes.

Steam or heat the tortillas. Grease a casserole and place a thin layer of tortillas on the bottom. Add a layer of turkey filling from the skillet. Repeat, ending with a thin layer of filling. Sprinkle the shredded cheese over the top and bake for 10 minutes, or until the cheese is melted nicely. Serve directly from the casserole dish, and top each serving with sour cream and shredded lettuce.

Variation: If you want to take a shortcut, make the filling by heating together 2 cups of prepared salsa and 2 cups of turkey. Add ¼ cup of cilantro if you have it, or substitute chopped celery tops.

TEN

Sauces, Dressings, and Go-withs

I don't want to bog down here in a hairsplitting discussion of what's stuffing and what's dressing. But I'll have to say that the culinary world would be a little better off if every recipe writer in the land used "stuffing" to stuff something and "dressing" to be cooked separately and piled along beside whatever is to be dressed. Unfortunately, the words are often used interchangeably. Some of the mixtures are indeed used to stuff and others are indeed used to dress. Some dishes work nicely either way, but of course must be cooked differently in each case, as noted in some of the recipes below.

This chapter also covers some commonly used side dishes and condiments, which can be especially important with turkey. No Thanksgiving roast turkey dinner, for example, is complete without cranberry sauce and giblet gravy.

Venison Sausage and Chestnut Stuffing

At one time, wild chestnuts were available over much of North America, but the trees were pretty much wiped out by a blight. A few trees remain today, and maybe one day they will regain their former numbers. Meanwhile, hunters and foragers will have to use cultivated chestnuts, which are available either fresh or canned. Fresh chestnuts should be boiled until tender, hulled, and chopped for the recipe. Canned chestnuts are precooked but should be chopped.

Any good sausage can be used in this stuffing, but many hunters will want to use their own venison sausage. Bulk sausage works best, but link sausage can be broken up and chopped.

> 8 cups crumbs from day-old bread (with crust removed)
> 1 cup chestnuts, chopped
> ½ pound venison sausage, cooked
> 2 slices bacon
> 1 medium onion, chopped
> 1 stalk celery with tops, chopped
> 2 tablespoons chopped fresh parsley
> 1 teaspoon chopped fresh thyme
> 5 juniper berries, crushed
> salt and pepper to taste

Fry the bacon in a skillet until crisp. Drain and crumble. In the bacon drippings sauté the sausage until done. (If you are using link sausage, break it up into small pieces.) Add the onion, celery, parsley, thyme, crushed juniper berries, chestnuts, salt, and pepper, and stir for several minutes, or until the onions are tender. Add the bread crumbs and mix well. Stuff the turkey with this mixture shortly before roasting.

Note: The juniper berries can be left out, but they do add to the flavor and add a historical note for the table talk. (See Juniper Berries and Sauce later in this chapter.)

Corn Bread and Giblet Stuffing

I normally prefer to save the giblets for gravy, but I'll have to admit that giblet stuffing is very tasty. Of course, you can save and freeze giblets from other turkeys, pheasants, or even small game birds like quail and doves. Even chickens have good giblets—and coots have a large gizzard that should always be saved. Remember, however, that the gizzard is normally tough and should be boiled longer than the liver.

Basically, all you do is boil the gizzard, heart, and neck, along with a bay leaf, until tender. Dice the gizzard and heart finely and return to the pot along with the liver. While the liver is cooking, pull the meat from the neck, chop it, and add it to the pot. Throw out the bay leaf. Drain the giblets. Save the broth. The recipe below calls for 2 cups of giblets, but use a little more if you've got them or a little less if you are short. If you alter the measure very much, however, make adjustments to the other ingredients.

> 2 cups giblets, boiled and chopped as above
> 4 cups corn bread, crumbled
> 1 stalk of celery with tops, chopped
> 1 medium onion, chopped
> 1/4 cup chopped fresh parsley
> giblet broth
> 1 teaspoon sage
> salt and pepper to taste
> 4 tablespoons bacon drippings

Heat the bacon drippings in a skillet and sauté the onion, parsley, and celery for 5 minutes. In a large bowl, mix the crumbled corn bread, giblets, onion mixture, sage, salt, and pepper. Stir in a little of the giblet broth—just enough to moisten the corn bread crumbs. Stuff the bird, and start cooking it immediately.

Pennsylvania Dutch Turkey Stuffing

Here's a basic recipe that will stuff a wild turkey of about 10 pounds. It is tasty, especially when topped with giblet gravy—and it's quite inexpensive compared with some of the oyster stuffings.

> 3 cups hot mashed potatoes
> 6 cups dry bread cubes
> 2 chicken eggs, beaten
> 1/4 cup butter
> 1/4 cup chopped fresh parsley
> 1 medium onion, chopped
> 1 teaspoon poultry seasoning
> salt and black pepper to taste

Beat the eggs and mix them into the mashed potatoes. Heat the butter in a skillet and sauté the bread cubes, then mix the cubes into the mashed potatoes. Mix in the other ingredients, stirring well.

Mushroom Stuffing

This recipe makes enough stuffing to fill a large wild turkey. Leftovers can be cooked in a casserole dish and served as dressing.

> 3 cups corn bread, crumbled
> 3 cups white bread, shredded
> 8 ounces fresh mushrooms, sliced
> 1 stalk celery with tops, chopped
> 1 medium onion, chopped
> $1/4$ cup chopped parsley
> $1/2$ cup butter or margarine
> 2 cups turkey or chicken stock
> $1/2$ teaspoon thyme
> salt and pepper to taste

Melt the butter or margarine in a skillet. Sauté mushrooms, onion, parsley, and celery for 5 minutes. Stir in the turkey stock, thyme, salt, and pepper. Bring to a boil. Add bread crumbs and mix well. Add a little more water if the stuffing seems too dry.

Corn Bread for Stuffing or Dressing

Really good corn bread, in my opinion, is made with meal milled from whole-grain corn. This meal has a higher oil content, and it doesn't store well for long periods of time. Naturally, the nation's large milling companies wanted a meal with a longer shelf life, and over the years they have altered the product greatly. Fortunately, a few pockets in the southern states and Rhode Island have held on to the old ways and the whole-grain meals. Today, stone-ground meals from small, local mills seem to be making a comeback. I buy mine in 10-pound bags and store it in the freezer.

I usually prefer a fine-ground white meal for corn pone and

hush puppies, but for the recipe below a medium grind works better. Either white or yellow will do. I have also tried stone-ground purple meal from the Southwest, but somehow the color of the stuffing turns me off.

> 2 cups medium-grind cornmeal
> 2 large chicken eggs
> 1 1/4 cups whole milk
> 1/4 cup Crisco
> 1 tablespoon baking powder
> 1/2 teaspoon baking soda
> 3/4 teaspoon salt

Preheat the oven to 425 degrees. In a bowl, mix the meal, baking powder, baking soda, and salt. Whisk the eggs lightly and add them to the meal, along with the milk and shortening. Beat the mixture until it is smooth, then pour it into a well-greased baking pan. (I almost always use my cast-iron skillet.)

Bake for 20 to 25 minutes, or until nicely browned. Crumble for use in stuffing.

Bread Dressing

This is a mild, all-purpose stuffing and dressing, perfect for eating with giblet gravy. Add other seasonings if you wish, such as sage or crushed juniper berries.

> 2 cups crumbled corn bread
> 1 cup crumbled biscuits
> 1 cup shredded white bread
> 2 stalks celery with tops, chopped
> 1 medium onion, chopped (about 1 cup)
> juice of 2 large lemons
> 1 cup butter
> 1 teaspoon salt
> 1/4 teaspoon cayenne
> 1 tablespoon white-wine Worcestershire sauce

Mix all ingredients except the butter in a large bowl. Melt the butter and mix it in. For a dressing, grease an oblong pan, put the mixture into it, and bake at 350 degrees for about an hour, or until it starts to brown on top. For a stuffing, stuff the bird loosely and cook according to the directions given in chapter 2.

Louisiana Oyster Stuffing

I got this recipe from *The Official Louisiana Seafood & Wild Game Cookbook,* and, of course, the list of ingredients calls for Louisiana oysters. I hold that oysters from Apalachicola, Florida, are better, but I am sure that other sports will champion fat mollusks from Chesapeake Bay or Puget Sound. In any case, this recipe makes a very good stuffing, not only because of the oysters but also because of the French bread.

> 1 loaf stale French bread
> 2 dozen large Louisiana oysters (and juice from shells)
> 1 cup cornmeal
> 1 cup chopped turkey liver
> 1/2 cup chopped pecans
> 3 medium onions, chopped
> 2 stalks celery with tops, chopped
> 2 chicken eggs, lightly beaten
> 1 tablespoon butter
> 1 teaspoon paprika
> 1 teaspoon crushed thyme
> 1/8 teaspoon sage
> salt and black pepper to taste

Cut the stale French bread in half lengthwise, and pour the oyster juice on either side. Then pull out large chunks of white bread, leaving the hard crust, and squeeze the juice from it with your hands. Put the chunks into a large mixing bowl and stir in the cornmeal. Heat the butter in a skillet and sauté the onions, celery, chopped liver, pecans, thyme, paprika, and sage until the onions are transparent. Add the bread mixture, salt, and pepper.

Chop the oysters into quarters and add to the stuffing. Turn off the heat and stir in the eggs. Stuff the turkey and cook it right away.

Oyster Dressing

The previous recipe was designed for stuffing a turkey. Here's an oyster recipe for cooking and serving separately. The list of ingredients calls for seasoned bread crumbs, such as Progresso Italian, available in most supermarkets.

> 1 quart oysters with liquid from shells
> 5 cups dry Italian bread crumbs
> 2 chicken eggs, lightly beaten
> 1 cup butter
> 3 medium onions, chopped
> 20 green onions with half of tops, chopped
> 2 stalks celery with tops, chopped
> 2 bell peppers, seeded and chopped
> 1/2 cup chopped fresh parsley
> salt and pepper to taste

Melt the butter in a large skillet, and sauté the onions, green onions, celery, and bell peppers for 20 minutes. Increase the heat and add the oysters and liquid from the shells. Stir for 20 minutes, then reduce the heat to medium and stir in the bread crumbs and eggs, along with some salt and pepper. Stir in the parsley. The mixture should be quite moist but not runny. If necessary, add either more bread crumbs or a little water to adjust the consistency. Lightly grease a 3- or 4-quart casserole or baking dish, and preheat the oven to 350 degrees. Dump the dressing into the dish and level it off roughly. Bake in the preheated oven until the mixture starts to bubble nicely. Cool and serve along with roasted turkey.

Easy Oyster and Cracker Stuffing

Somehow, oysters and saltine crackers seem to go together, either raw or cooked. I remember, for example, when my mother coated

145

raw oysters in crushed cracker crumbs and fried them. My problem is that I love raw oysters on crackers so much, and my shucking is so slow, that I might never accumulate a full pint.

    1 box crackers (16-ounce size)
    1 pint oysters with juice
    1 cup butter, melted
    1 medium onion, chopped
    1 stalk celery with tops, chopped
    2 teaspoons sage
    1 teaspoon black pepper

Crumble the crackers into a mixing bowl and sprinkle with sage and pepper. Toss in the chopped celery and onion, then stir in the melted butter, oysters, and liquid from the shells. Stuff the bird and cook right away.

Variation: Add about 8 ounces of sliced mushrooms and some chopped parsley.

Wild Rice

Several misconceptions about wild rice should be cleared up. Real rice is a grain; wild rice is the seed of an aquatic grass, *Zizania aquatica* and related species, such as *Zizania texana,* which grows in Texas.

Wild rice grows widely in North America, not just in the upper Midwest, and it is harvested commercially in several states. Wild rice will grow in brackish as well as fresh water. It has been planted as food for ducks and other wildlife, in which case harvesting a little for the table won't hurt a thing; in fact, moderate harvesting may cause the wild rice to expand faster. Surprisingly, there are several varieties of wild rice and several different grades; some "wild rice" is actually cultivated in irrigated ponds in California and harvested by machine. Some varieties have a short grain, others long, and still others in between. The size also varies from one individual grain to another, so grading is required for rice that is marketed.

No foolproof rules can be set forth here, but be warned that some kinds of wild rice require more water and a much longer cooking time than others. In all cases, wild rice requires more water and a longer cooking time than real rice. If you purchase commercially packaged wild rice, be sure to follow the directions on the box or bag. If you gather your own, you should proceed with what I call a ballpark recipe, as follows:

> 1 cup wild rice
> 3 cups water
> salt to taste

Rinse the wild rice in cold water and drain. Put it into a suitable pan, cover it with 3 cups of water, and add the salt. Bring to a quick boil. Reduce the heat, cover, and simmer for 30 minutes. Check the water level and test the rice. Add water as needed, and cook until the grains are tender—which may take up to an hour altogether.

One cup of wild rice when fully cooked will expand greatly, yielding from 3 to 4 cups.

Helen's Rice

There are several ways of cooking rice. I prefer it to be fluffy, so that each piece can be separated from the others, unless I am trying to eat with chopsticks, in which case sticky rice is required. My good wife is the rice expert in our household, and she cooks it by a very simple but exact method.

First, get a small pot with a tight lid. Grease the bottom and sides with a little butter or margarine or, perhaps, a chunk of salt pork. Pour in exactly 3 cups of water. Add a little salt. Bring to a hard boil. Add exactly 1½ cups of long-grain rice. Bring to a new boil, cover, reduce heat, and simmer for exactly 20 minutes. Do not under any circumstances take the lid off the rice during cooking. After 20 minutes, remove the pot from the heat and dip the bottom into some cold water. For dipping, you can use a larger pot full of water, or you can plug up the sink and catch some water in it. (You can tilt the rice pan a little and hold it under the cold water tap, if your wife isn't looking—or dip the bottom of the pan into the creek if you are in camp.)

Giblet Gravy

Giblet gravy is usually served on the table along with a roast turkey and other trimmings, and many people put it onto slices of turkey breast. If the breast isn't cooked too long, however, I prefer to use the gravy atop a serving of dressing or stuffing. Suit yourself—but don't fail to make gravy, using this recipe or your own favorite. The term "giblets" usually includes the liver, gizzard, heart, and neck. I also include the wing tips and feet, which add flavor to the stock.

Be sure that the gizzard is dressed properly. It should be cut open with a sharp knife, turned inside out, and peeled.

> wild turkey giblets
> 1 stalk celery with tops
> 1 small onion (golf-ball size)
> 1 hard-boiled chicken egg
> 1/4 cup butter or margarine
> salt and pepper
> 1 bay leaf (optional)
> 1/4 cup flour
> water

Wash the giblets and put the neck, feet, heart, and dressed gizzard into a saucepan of suitable size and cover with water. Add a little salt and a bay leaf. Bring to a boil, reduce heat, cover, and simmer for at least an hour, or until the gizzard is tender. Remove all the turkey pieces and discard the feet and wing tips. Dice the gizzard and heart into small pieces and put them back into the pot. Pull the meat off the neck as best you can, chop it, and put it back into the pot. Chop the liver and add it to the pot, bring to a new boil, cover, and simmer for 20 minutes or so. Meanwhile, finely chop the celery and onion, including the celery tops. Make a paste of the flour and a little water. Heat butter or margarine in an 11-inch cast-iron skillet. Sauté the onion and celery, then slowly add the flour paste, stirring as you go with a wooden spoon. Stir in the broth from the pot, then chop the liver and add it and the other chopped giblets to the frying pan. Stir and simmer for a few minutes. When the gravy is almost ready to serve, chop the hard-boiled egg and carefully stir it into the gravy. Pour into a gravy bowl and serve with the roast turkey, dressing, and other trimmings that go along with a whole roast turkey.

Note, however, that this gravy can be used in other ways. I like it spooned over mashed potatoes or rice, served along with, perhaps, grilled turkey fingers. I also like giblet gravy served on toast for lunch or on biscuit halves for breakfast.

Backwoods Turkey Pilau

The people of rural Florida, especially in and around the Big Scrub area, cook a rice dish, usually called purloo, with chicken, turkey, squirrel, and other good meats. It is seasoned to taste with salt and pepper. Many people like the distinctive taste of red pepper flakes instead of black pepper. In hard times, purloo is served as a main meal, but often it is served as a side dish for a Sunday dinner. It is also popular at large gatherings, such as family reunions or church dinners. Essentially, the dish contains meat, rice, and water, but some people add chopped onions and even tomatoes. The recipe below calls for the frame of a wild turkey, which would include what's left after the breasts have been filleted out and the hind-quarters disjointed. You can also use the drumsticks and other parts of the turkey. The exact measure of the meat is not critical, but reasonable proportions should be maintained.

> turkey frame
> water
> 1 large onion
> salt and red pepper flakes
> 2 bay leaves (optional)
> 1 cup uncooked long-grain rice

Put the turkey frame into a pot of suitable size (I usually use a Dutch oven) and pour in 3 cups of water. Add the chopped onion, salt, bay leaves, and red pepper flakes. (The bay leaves are optional, but I like them because they give a nice aroma to the kitchen while the meat is boiling. In fact, I almost always use a bay leaf or two with boiled meats.) Bring to a boil, reduce heat, cover, and simmer for 1 hour, or until the turkey meat pulls off the bone easily. Remove the turkey frame. Pull the meat off the bone and chop it. Throw out the bay leaf and measure out 3 cups of the broth. If you don't have 3 cups, add some water. Put the broth back into the pot and add the chopped turkey. Bring to a boil, put in the rice, reduce heat, and simmer for 25 minutes. Remove the lid from the pot and simmer very slowly until the rice is almost dry and grainy, if that's the way you want the dish. If it is to be used as a side dish, it should be on the dry side so that it won't run all over the plate. On the other hand, it can be on the soupy side if eaten from a bowl; serve along with saltines or bread. I like it both ways—and I usually call the side dish pilau and the soupy kind purloo. Suit yourself.

Pilau is always good in camp, and the measures above can be increased to feed a large crowd. Apart from a reasonable amount of meat, the critical ratio is 3 cups of broth for every 1 cup of dry long-grain rice. I acknowledge that the usual ratio for water to rice is 2 to 1, but remember that the broth is thicker than water.

Cranberry Sauce

Roast turkey and cranberry sauce have become something of a tradition in America, and the two do indeed complement each other very well. The hunter who bags his own wild turkey can, in some areas, gather his own wild cranberries for sauce. Also, fresh cranberries are available at supermarkets all over the country during the Thanksgiving and Christmas holidays, and these can be frozen for use all year.

16 ounces fresh cranberries
1¼ cups sugar
1¼ cups water

Put the water and sugar into a saucepan, stir, and bring to a boil. Add the cranberries, bring to a new boil, reduce heat, and simmer for 10 minutes, stirring every 2 minutes or so, or until the cranberries pop open. Let the mixture cool a bit, pour it into a serving dish of suitable shape to form a mold, and refrigerate until ready to serve.

Variation: The Indians and early settlers in the Northeast used maple sugar instead of white sugar. Try a half-and-half mix.

Cranberry Orange Relish

I usually prefer ordinary cranberry sauce with turkey, but some people will want something a little more fancy. Here's a good one with nuts and an orange flavor.

> 16 ounces fresh or fresh-frozen cranberries
> 2 cups sugar
> 1/2 cup blanched almonds, slivered
> 1/2 cup fresh orange juice
> 1/2 cup water
> 2 teaspoons grated orange rind

Using a fine mesh, grate 2 teaspoons of orange peeling from the outside, avoiding the inner white pith, which is bitter. Mix all the ingredients except the almonds in a saucepan, bring to a boil, reduce heat, and simmer for 10 minutes, or until the cranberries pop open. Remove from heat and skim the scum off the surface with a spoon. Stir in the almonds, pour into a serving container, and refrigerate until time to eat.

Applesauce

My mother often served a bowl of applesauce with a Thanksgiving or Christmas feast. It somehow made dry turkey breast go down nicely and also seemed to lighten the load of eating too much rich stuffing. The only problem was finding a place to put it on your plate. In any case, I recommend applesauce with roasted turkey. Try this recipe.

3 pounds cooking apples
$\frac{1}{2}$ cup sugar
$\frac{1}{2}$ cup water
$\frac{1}{8}$ teaspoon cinnamon
$\frac{1}{8}$ teaspoon ground cloves

Peel, core, and slice the apples. Bring the water to a boil and add the apples, cinnamon, and ground cloves. Reduce heat, cover, and simmer for 10 minutes. Stir in the sugar and cook for another 3 or 4 minutes. If the sauce is too lumpy to suit you, mash it with a potato masher and cook for another 2 or 3 minutes. Chill until feasting time.

Kumquat Sauce

I like this sauce served with sliced turkey. Being rather tart, it adds zest to a bland meal. It's best to wash the kumquats and slice them rather thinly crosswise, removing the seeds as you go.

2 cups sliced kumquats
$1\frac{1}{2}$ cups water
$\frac{1}{4}$ cup honey

Put the sliced kumquats and water into a saucepan. Bring to a boil and stir in the honey. Reduce heat and simmer for 30 minutes.

Pomegranate Syrup

The peoples in the Middle East are fond of a red syrup made of pomegranate juice and sugar. (It is similar to the original grenadine used in bartending, but these days most of the bottled grenadine on the market doesn't contain pomegranate juice.) This syrup is often used as a sweet-sour sauce for fish and poultry. The recipe below is fairly standard, and the sweetness can be altered by the amount of sugar used.

On the farm where I was raised, we had several pomegranate trees, and the fruit is now raised commercially in this country. It is available, in the fall, in supermarkets. Sometimes the super-market pomegranates are quite large, so the number used in this recipe may need to be reduced.

> 8 medium pomegranates (about the size of a baseball)
> $^1/_2$ cup sugar

Peel the pomegranates and separate the seeds. Put the seeds into a fruit press and squeeze out the juice. A bag made from muslin will work. Be warned that the juice will stain your clothing. Put the juice into a non-aluminum saucepan. Stir in the sugar and turn on the heat. Stir constantly until the sugar melts and the liquid reaches a boil. Quickly reduce the heat, skim off any foam, and simmer lightly until the mixture reduces to about half its original volume. Remove from the heat, cool, and pour into a sterilized jar. Store in the refrigerator.

The pomegranate syrup can be used as an accompaniment to sliced turkey. I like it especially with grilled turkey, and I use it as a baste during the last few minutes of cooking. If you like mixed drinks, try this beautiful homemade syrup in any recipe that calls for grenadine.

Wild Plum Sauce

The Chinese enjoy a plum sauce with meat, and the peoples of the Caucasus (especially Georgia) make a "sour plum" sauce for use with turkey, chicken, and other meat. My mother also made a tart plum sauce from the wild plums that grew around the edge of our farm. The following recipe can be used with either wild or domestic plums.

> 1 quart wild plums
> water
> 3 tablespoons chopped cilantro (or Chinese parsley)
> 1 tablespoon freshly chopped basil
> $^1/_4$ teaspoon salt
> $^1/_4$ teaspoon Tabasco sauce

Put the plums into a boiler and add enough water to almost cover them. Bring to a boil, reduce heat, cover, and simmer for about 20 minutes, or until the plums are soft. Remove the plums, and set aside the boiler and liquid. Remove the pits from the plums and put the fruits into a blender or food processor. Add a little liquid from the boiler. Zap the mixture and add a little more of the liquid from the boiler. Continue until you have a thick sauce. Put this sauce into the liquid in the boiler. Stir in the cilantro, basil, salt, and Tabasco sauce. Serve with grilled, broiled, or roasted turkey.

Sweet Wild Plum Sauce

If the recipe above doesn't suit your fancy, here's a way to make a simple plum sauce with some sugar in it. Use ripe but not mushy wild or cultivated plums. Wash the plums and put them into a saucepan of suitable size. Cover with sugar, stirring so that the sugar settles. Using a potato masher, work the plums enough to get a juice on the bottom. Heat slowly, stirring from time to time, until the mixture thickens. Mash the mixture through a sieve to remove the seeds and skins. Serve chilled. This sauce can be kept under refrigeration for several weeks.

Honey Mustard Sauce

This sauce is just right with turkey egg rolls. Dry mustard can be found in the spice sections of supermarkets, but I like to grind my own from seeds as needed with the aid of a mortar and pestle. You can purchase these seeds, but anyone who raises mustard greens in the garden can get plenty of seeds just by letting the plants grow to maturity. Foragers might also try seeds from wild mustard.

> $1/4$ cup dry mustard
> 1 tablespoon honey
> 1 tablespoon peanut oil
> $1/4$ teaspoon salt
> $1/4$ cup water

Stir together the mustard, oil, honey, and salt in a serving bowl. Boil the water in a small pan and pour it slowly into the sauce, stirring as you go.

Cumberland Sauce

Here's a traditional sauce for spooning over fowl. It should be put on the table in suitable bowls for individual servings.

> $1/2$ cup red currant jelly
> 2 tablespoons prepared mustard
> 2 egg yolks
> $1/4$ cup port wine
> juice of 2 lemons
> 2 tablespoons sugar
> 1 tablespoon grated orange peel
> 1 teaspoon freshly grated ginger root
> salt and cayenne pepper to taste

Heat a little water in the bottom unit of a double boiler, and melt the jelly in the top. Take the double boiler off the heat and cool for 5 minutes. While waiting, grate the orange peel with a fine mesh, using only the outside part of the peeling; avoid the inner white part, which is bitter. Into the jelly, stir the egg yolks, mustard, ginger, orange, port, orange peel, lemon juice, sugar, salt, and cayenne. Remember that cayenne is very hot stuff, so a pinch will be sufficient for most tastes. Mix everything thoroughly, then put the top part of the double boiler directly onto the heat, and bring to a light boil. Reduce heat and simmer for 30 minutes, stirring frequently.

Variation: If you don't have red currant jelly at hand, try a tart plum jelly.

Colonial Oyster Sauce

When the settlers came to the eastern seaboard, they found plenty of oysters in the bays and quite a few turkeys in the forests. In addition to using the oysters along with breads for stuffing, they also used them to make a delicious hot sauce for turkey. These days, the price of oysters has gone sky high, but I usually manage to purchase a large burlap bag full in the fall, around Thanksgiving, for eating on the half shell. I also use some to shuck out a pint for the following recipe. I shuck the oyster directly into the pint container, a process that yields some good salty juice as well as the morsel. If you don't shuck your own, get them shucked fresh at your favorite oyster bar and watch the oysterman to see that he doesn't switch bucket oysters on you. But, of course, bucket oysters are better than no oysters at all.

> 1 pint oysters with some liquid
> $1/4$ cup butter
> $1/4$ cup all-purpose flour
> $1/2$ cup half and half
> juice of 1 small lemon
> $1/8$ teaspoon nutmeg
> sea salt
> white pepper

If you have freshly shucked oysters, forget the sea salt. If you have bucket oysters, which will have been washed, add a little sea salt to the liquid in the container. In either case, put the oysters into a small saucepan, bring to heat, and simmer for 5 minutes, or until the oysters curl, stirring all the while. Remove the pan from the heat and set aside.

In another saucepan or skillet, melt the butter and stir in the flour, nutmeg, salt, and white pepper. (The nutmeg has more flavor if you grate your own, in which case you grate it directly into the mixture instead of measuring it—and use it very sparingly.) Stir with a wooden spoon until the flour is well blended. Slowly stir in the half and half, cooking until it starts to bubble. Do not boil. Stir in the oysters (with all the pan juices) and the lemon juice. Serve the sauce hot, spooning it over carved turkey.

The colonists made several similar sauces, including one

for poached fish. You can make a good one by merely adding a little anchovy paste.

Salsa

This hot sauce can be used as a condiment, served in a bowl on the table so that each diner can take it or leave it. The sauce can also be used on tacos, turkey enchiladas, and the like. A good deal depends on what sort of green chili peppers you have on hand. Whether you use fresh or frozen, it's best to remove the seeds and inner pith unless you want the salsa to be hot to the extreme.

>2 cups fresh tomatoes, chopped
>2 hot green chilies
>1 medium onion, minced
>2 cloves garlic, minced
>1 tablespoon minced cilantro
>juice of 1 lime
>salt

Before proceeding, bring some water to a boil and scald the tomatoes. Then peel them, remove the stem part, and chop them. Put all ingredients into a saucepan, bring to a boil, reduce heat, and simmer for a few minutes. Chill and serve in a bowl.

Note: This recipe is also good when made with half red tomatoes and half Mexican green husk tomatoes.

Coconut Milk

The coconut is now used in one way or another in the cuisine of most parts of the world, and coconut milk is a very important ingredient in many recipes in Africa and Indonesia. Many people who purchase coconuts at the supermarket think that the liquid inside, drained out by punching through one of the eyes with an ice pick, is coconut milk. It isn't. To make milk, you first crack the coconut, remove the meat in chunks, and then grate it. Measure the grated meat and put it into a suitable container. Then pour over it an equal volume of steaming hot water. Let this steep until it is cool enough to squeeze the coconut meat in your hand. Then squeeze out the liquid and strain it. This is coconut milk. You can repeat the process several times, but note that the liquid will become weaker as you go. Thus, you can obtain weak or strong coconut milk—and you can even obtain "cream" by letting the strong milk stand for several hours and then skimming off the rich top layer. You can also obtain a richer coconut milk by using hot milk (real milk from a cow, yak, goat, water buffalo, or such) instead of water.

In order to obtain 1 cup of coconut milk, start with 1½ cups of grated meat and 1½ cups of hot water. Run more water through it for weaker milk; this can be used to advantage when cooking rice, which, I might add, usually goes with every Indonesian meal and with many African dishes.

If you don't want to bother with fresh grated coconut milk, you can substitute unsweetened desiccated grated coconut, available in packages at most supermarkets, or you may be able to find some canned or frozen coconut milk in supermarkets or specialty food stores. I have bought it by mail.

Fried Pumpkins

The Old World had various edible melons and gourds, but the squash and the pumpkin are from the New World. Of course, the pumpkin has become associated in the American mind with Thanksgiving, at which feast it is usually served in the form of pie. As fried fare also seems to be the American way, it is somewhat surprising that the following recipe for fried pumpkin should instead come our way from Armenia, where it is said to be popular with turkey.

> 2 pounds pumpkin, sliced
> 1 large onion, diced
> 1 cup butter
> salt
> sugar

Cut the pumpkin crosswise into slices about ³/₈ inch thick and trim off the rind and the seed fibers. (A large pumpkin can be cut in half or into quarters before slicing.) Retain 2 tablespoons of butter and heat the rest in a skillet. Sauté the pumpkin slices on both sides until they are nicely browned, then sprinkle them lightly with the salt and sugar. Transfer the slices to a heated serving platter. Melt the rest of the butter in the skillet, and stir-fry the onion until it is browned. Sprinkle the onions over the pumpkin and serve by slices.

Applejack Basting Sauce

I don't know the origin of this recipe, but I like to think it developed at the hearth in Colonial New England for basting a wild turkey on a spit.

> 2 cups apple cider
> 2 ounces applejack
> ¹/₂ cup butter
> ¹/₄ teaspoon tarragon

Mix everything in a saucepan of suitable size. Bring to a boil, reduce heat, and simmer for 5 minutes. Use warm as a basting sauce for grilled or broiled turkey.

Lemon Butter Basting Sauce

This easy sauce goes nicely with grilled or broiled turkey. If you want a smoke flavor, use the Liquid Smoke.

> ¹/₂ cup butter
> juice of 4 lemons
> 1 tablespoon Liquid Smoke
> 1 tablespoon white-wine Worcestershire sauce
> ¹/₂ tablespoon salt

Melt the butter in a saucepan, and stir in the other ingredients.

Mix well but do not boil. Use to baste broiled or grilled turkey breast meat.

Juniper Berries and Sauce

Juniper berries, now used to flavor gin, were important flavorings to the American Indians and early settlers. They can still be used to advantage today and go nicely with wild turkey and other game birds. Try a few, crushed, in your turkey stuffing or in stews and soups. Juniper berries, which are actually small cones instead of true berries, can be gathered in the wild, or they can sometimes be purchased in spice markets.

Although I usually use juniper berries like a spice, you may want to make a sauce for your wild turkey. Here's an excellent recipe from *Alaska Magazine's Cabin Cookbook.*

"Crush a few dried juniper berries between 2 sheets of waxed paper with a rolling pin. Make at least a couple of teaspoonsful. Then heat 2 tablespoons butter or margarine until light brown, but not scorched. Stir in 2 tablespoons flour and continue stirring over low heat for 2 or 3 minutes. Now add a cup of game stock or bouillon and simmer for 15 minutes longer, stirring now and then. Then add about ½ cup Madeira wine, salt and pepper to taste, and the crushed juniper berries and simmer for 10 more minutes. If the sauce is a bit too thick to suit you, just add a little more stock, a spoonful at a time."

Turkey Stock

This stock can be used in several of the recipes in this book or, in fact, in any recipe that calls for chicken stock. It is very, very good when used as a base for soups and stews. I make it from the turkey frame that's left after I fillet out the breast and disjoint the legs. If I bone out the thighs and drumsticks, these bones will go into the stock as well. The neck and feet can also be used to advantage. In any case, it's best to leave a little meat on the bones instead of picking them clean.

turkey frame and bones
water to cover
4 stalks celery with tops
4 carrots
4 medium onions
cloves
2 or 3 bay leaves
salt and pepper

Chop the celery and carrots. Peel the onions and stud each one with 2 cloves. Put all the ingredients into the pot and cover with water. Bring to a boil, reduce heat, cover, and simmer for 3 or 4 hours. Add a little water from time to time if needed. Strain the stock into jars. It will keep in the refrigerator for several days. For longer storage, freeze it.

I usually throw out what's left of the vegetables, but I do pull the turkey meat off the bones and use it in salads or other recipes that call for cooked turkey.

APPENDIX A

Ten Steps to Better Wild Turkey

The foregoing chapters set forth instructions and tips for cooking wild turkey by various methods. I won't repeat myself here, except to say that the meat thermometer can be the hunter's best friend whenever a bird is to be roasted whole. Here are some other points that can help make your wild turkey into a memorable meal.

1. Be a good hunter. With any wild game, it's best for the hunter to make a clean kill. An animal that dies under prolonged traumatic conditions will be tougher and not as toothsome as it could otherwise be. These days, most turkey hunters call the bird to them and shoot it in the head with a well-patterned shotgun. (The expert hunter must, of course, master the art of camouflage in addition to learning how to call the birds; he should also know how to pattern his gun and find exactly the right load for his particular gun.) This method of hunting is ideal for putting meat on the table, because a shot or two in the head usually results in a quick kill. Also, shooting at the head with a tight pattern won't normally leave bird shot embedded in the carcass and won't tear up the meat like a rifle bullet into the breast area.

2. Field dressing. It's best to draw your bird as soon as possible after the kill. The purpose is not so much to remove the innards per se, as most people believe, but to remove the heat that they contain and to open a cavity to permit quicker cooling of the carcass.

Remove the innards from the rear. Start by plucking away the small feathers between the end of the breastbone and the vent. Make a shallow cut through the skin, being careful not to cut into the innards. (If you plan to stuff the bird, it's best to keep the opening as small as possible.) Reach in with your hand and remove the innards. Then reach in deeper and detach the lungs and tubes leading into the throat. After removing all the innards, sort out the heart, liver, and gizzard if you want them for giblet gravy. Be sure to remove, very carefully, the bitter gall sac from the liver; it's better to slice off a small part of the liver in order to avoid puncturing this sac, which will ruin the liver and possibly the other giblets. Put these parts aside to cool.

Next, make an opening at the point where the neck joins the crop, just in front of the breast. Remove any undigested food matter in the crop. Again, keep the opening as small as possible if you intend to stuff the bird.

Keep the bird in a cool, airy place until you are ready to pluck or skin it. If you have taken the bird on a hot day, as may often be the case during the spring or fall seasons in Florida, you might consider either skinning or plucking the bird as part of the field-dressing operation. Removing the feathers will help cool the meat. Skin or pluck the bird before dumping out the innards. (See the next step.)

If you have a large ice chest, put the bird in it atop a bed of ice. It's best to keep the water drained out.

3. Plucking or skinning. I prefer to pluck a bird, because I think the skin helps hold in the juices during cooking or storage. This is especially important when you are roasting a whole bird. Also, any bird that is to be stuffed should be plucked. If you are going to grill or fry turkey fingers, the skin isn't too important and can be pulled off or left on. Suit yourself.

If you pluck the bird in the field or dry pluck it at home, it's best to hang it by the feet and pull the body feathers against the grain, so to speak. The wing quills can cause some problems, and the larger ones come out better if you use a good set of pliers. After plucking the bird, go over it with tweezers, pulling out the pin feathers embedded in the skin, and then singe the body. The singeing can be accomplished by loosely rolling a couple of sheets of newspaper, lighting the end, and working the flame around the suspended bird.

If I field-dress the bird, I am usually in no hurry to pluck it, except, perhaps, in hot weather. In fact, I have kept a bird for several days in the refrigerator with the skin and feathers on—and for several months in the freezer. But the feathers come out easier if you pluck the bird while it's still warm.

It's a little easier to wet pluck the bird, by first immersing it in a large pot of hot water. Of course, putting the bird into a pot of boiling water for very long will partly cook it. For that reason, it's best to wet the bird thoroughly with cold or warm water, then immerse it in water of about 200 degrees for no longer than a minute.

If you are going to skin the bird, it's best to hang it by the head. Cut around the neck and start working the skin down. I also cut off the wing tip before I start skinning the bird. The feet can also be removed prior to skinning, but save them for stock, if you are so inclined. (If you are having culinary sports or a Frenchman over for dinner, be sure to use the feet in stock or gravy and mention the *abatis de dinde en fricassée au blanc* during your table talk. But consider your guests carefully before resorting to this bit of showmanship. Some people simply don't care for turkey feet, French-cooked or otherwise.)

4. Aging. If a wild turkey has been promptly field-dressed and cooled, I like to age the meat for a couple of days in the refrigerator before grilling or frying it. This makes the meat a little more tender. If you do plan to age the bird, leave the skin on it.

Freezing the bird properly for a couple of weeks will also help cure the meat. See the next step.

5. Freezing and thawing. If you freeze a bird whole, it's usually best to pluck it instead of skinning it. (In rare cases, you may choose to freeze a whole bird in a block of ice, in which case a skinned bird would do.) Wrap the bird carefully in freezer paper before putting it into the freezer. I like to chill mine first in the refrigerator, if I've got room, then put it into an isolated portion of the freezer until it is frozen hard. Note that putting a warm bird next to small packages of frozen food may thaw them. If you've got more than one bird to freeze, or venison as well as turkey, it's best to freeze only part of it at a time. You might also consider taking the batch to a meat processor for quick freezing before storing it in your home freezer.

If you are certain of how you will cook the bird, you may consider disjointing the carcass and freezing parts of the turkey separately. Fillets from the breast, for example, make nice pieces of meat that wrap and store easily. You can even disjoint the bird and freeze the parts in water (milk cartons work nicely). As a rule, turkey frozen in water keeps better and longer than pieces that have been wrapped. I usually freeze the giblets in water.

Always mark the contents of the container or package, noting carefully the kind of meat being frozen, weight, date, and so on. (When reading the first draft of this book, my wife underlined the last statement three times.)

Most authorities recommend that a turkey, or other large chunks of meat, be thawed in the refrigerator. I agree in principle, but in practice this sometimes takes too long and isn't practical. I have thawed a large gobbler in the kitchen sink, and I hereby plead guilty of running lukewarm water over him to speed the process. Some people have even thawed turkeys in a microwave—but I seldom go that far.

6. Choose an appropriate method of cooking. An old bird, whether it be a pheasant or a chicken or a turkey, is simply not tender. As a rule, however, an old hen is not as tough as an old tom or rooster. With turkey, the jakes and first-year hens usually make the best eating. These can be cooked by any method and are delicious when fried. Older birds should be stewed or steamed. (I consider a bird that is wrapped tightly in foil, or put into a baking bag, and cooked in the oven or indirectly on a grill to be partly steamed instead of merely roasted or grilled.) As a rule, the longer a tough bird is stewed or steamed, the more succulent it will be, but the inverse is true with any dry method of cooking—true baking, broiling, or grilling. If you've got a really tough bird, remember that the crockpot is about as foolproof as any method of cooking can be.

Also, choose a method of cooking to suit the occasion. While I was putting the finishing touches on this book, for example, our grown boys and son-in-law all gathered for the Christmas holidays, and I considered various ways of cooking. It was a special time for us, and we also had a crowd from my wife's side of the family coming in. In short, I figured we would need lots of meat and lots of trimmings. I decided to cook the meat out in the yard and let my wife have the kitchen. The weather turned too cold for comfortable patio cooking, so I decided that a bonfire and a cooking pit would be in order. The day before Christmas, the boys dug the hole enthusiastically, making it a little larger than my specifications, and gathered plenty of good oak wood. At first dark we lit the fire. It was nice for us to stand around the pit, warming first one side and then the other, and tell stories of times gone by. We even rigged a grill across one end of the hole and roasted fresh oysters. At about midnight, when the fire had burned down to a bed of glowing coals, I wrapped a whole turkey and a 10-pound sirloin tip in heavy aluminum foil, lowered them into the pit, and covered them up with the dirt that came out of the hole.

The next morning, about an hour before noon, we dug the meat out and brought it in for the womenfolks to finish. I would be less than honest if I didn't say here that the primary method of cooking didn't work as planned and the meat wasn't done. My good wife came to the rescue, zapping the meat in a microwave oven. Of course, the boys had a belly laugh at the old man's expense. I told 'em, hell, I didn't dig the hole. But it all turned out to be a wonderful meal, with plenty of meat and good cheer. I wouldn't want to change it.

But I wouldn't build a bonfire and open a keg of beer if I were young and courting and had bagged a wild turkey for my lady love. Candlelight and champagne would be in order. I would pepper some exquisite tenderloins of turkey breast, broil them in butter, and flame them with brandy.

7. Be a painstaking cook. The secret to good cooking lies not in recipes but in careful attention to detail. Of course, good recipes and top-quality ingredients are very important, but they guarantee nothing. In fact, I consider the selection of appropriate recipes and quality ingredients as part of being a good cook. Don't skimp. Freshly ground pepper has more flavor and aroma. Fresh garlic is superior to powdered garlic. Little things count.

Remember that wild turkey should not be overcooked, especially when you are roasting or grilling or broiling it by direct heat.

166

This statement is true of most game, which tends to be lean and a little tough as compared with feedlot cattle or chicken-house fryers. To cook a wild turkey too long is a culinary sin. If you bake the turkey in the oven, get a good meat thermometer and learn how to use it. Expensive oyster dressing won't help a dehydrated turkey.

8. Fowlmanship. Although it is natural for a hunter to take pride in his bird, it might be best, in some cases, to refrain from putting the whole thing on the table for everybody to see. It is much easier to carve the bird on the kitchen counter than on the table, which might well be cluttered with food and drink. In any case, a good carbon steel knife (which is usually ugly) will usually do a better job, if it is properly sharpened, than a stainless steel knife or other cutlery designed for use at the dining table.

Carving the bird before putting it onto the table speeds things up considerably and makes for a smoother dinner. If you want to display the bird, at least consider carving some slices off one side to get things started. If you are a good showman, however, you might turn the carving ceremony to your advantage. Just make sure you know what you are doing. And always be ready for accidents at the board. I recall a written piece by the late H. Allen Smith in which the bird (either a turkey or a goose) slipped, scooted off the platter, and plopped down into the lap of one of the ladies at the table. "Madam," the host said, "I'll thank you for that fowl!"

9. Meal planning. A friend of mine likes to cook a complicated shrimp dish with lots of olive oil and garlic. With this dish he takes great pains, and he is proud of the result. He wants to serve it with rice, French-type bread, and a Greek salad, all of which complement the dish perfectly. His wife, however, manages to put all manner of stuff on the table with it. She is also a very good cook, but the two styles just don't fit together. She leans toward the big spread for company, whereas he wants a specialty dish and plenty of it. I side with him.

I have seen the same sort of thing happen in other households. Once, when we were to feed a crowd from my wife's side of the family, we planned something different. For one thing, I don't like a big meal at 11:00 in the morning. (Most of the big family dinners on that side of the family are started early in the morning, and the womenfolks want to eat early so that they can wash the dishes and, in general, "get through with it.") For another thing, a meal ought to have a theme. For example, a New England boiled dinner, made with corned venison and boiled cabbage and potatoes and carrots and turnip roots, doesn't benefit from having fried catfish on the table, even if you are dining in Mississippi.

Always consider your guests before planning a meal. If some of them might be squeamish about wild meat, you should feel confident that your bird and your skill as a chef will change their minds. On the other hand, you won't want to turn them off before they even taste your bird. Therefore, grilled or fried turkey fingers might be a better choice than a whole bird displayed in the center of the table.

10. Gather kindred spirits. During ancient times, a feast often followed a successful hunt. Although the tradition has declined during our century, the ultimate fulfillment for the hunter comes at the table. There is—or can be—something special, something memorable, about a good dinner either at home or at the hunting lodge. But meat alone isn't enough. As Marjorie Kinnan Rawlings said at the end of her book *Cross Creek Cooking*, "Two elements enter into successful and happy gatherings at the table. The food, whether it be simple or elaborate, must be carefully prepared; willingly prepared; imaginatively prepared. And the guests— friends, family, or strangers—must be conscious of their welcome."

I would add that the guests must also want to be at the table and should not be at great odds on the subject of meat and hunting. It's difficult, to say the least, for a stringy, antihunting vegetarian and a pot-bellied, hungry good ol' boy to eat, drink, and be merry while looking at each other over a stuffed wild turkey. It is therefore important to choose one's guests carefully, if, indeed, one has a choice. Since preparing and eating fish and game for the table count among the finer things in my life, I hereby give thanks and say grace for my good wife, our children, and my friends. Amen—and pass the wild turkey.

APPENDIX B

Metric Conversion Tables

U.S. Standard measurements for cooking use ounces, pounds, pints, quarts, gallons, teaspoons, tablespoons, cups, and fractions thereof. The following tables enable those who use the metric system to easily convert the U.S. Standard measurements to metric.

Weights

U.S. Standard	Metric	U.S. Standard		Metric
.25 ounce	7.09 grams	11	ounces	312 grams
.50	14.17	12		340
.75	21.26	13		369
1	28.35	14		397
2	57	15		425
3	85	1	pound	454
4	113	2		907
5	142	2.2		1 kilogram
6	170	4.4		2
7	198	6.6		3
8	227	8.8		4
9	255	11.0		5
10	283			

Liquids

U.S. Standard	Metric	U.S. Standard	Metric
¹/₈ teaspoon	.61 milliliter	³/₈ cup	90 milliliters
¹/₄	1.23	¹/₂	120
¹/₂	2.50	²/₃	160
³/₄	3.68	³/₄	180
1	4.90	⁷/₈	210
2	10	1	240
1 tablespoon	15	2	480
2	30	3	720
¹/₄ cup	60	4	960
¹/₃	80	5	1200

To convert	multiply	by
Ounces to milliliters	the ounces	30
Teaspoons to milliliters	the teaspoons	5
Tablespoons to milliliters	the tablespoons	15
Cups to liters	the cups	.24
Pints to liters	the pints	.47
Quarts to liters	the quarts	.95
Gallons to liters	the gallons	3.8
Ounces to grams	the ounces	28.35
Pounds to kilograms	the pounds	.45
Inches to centimeters	the inches	2.54

To convert Fahrenheit to Celsius: Subtract 32, multiply by 5, divide by 9.

Index

A. D.'s Armadillo Eggs, 128–30
A. D.'s Fried Turkey Fingers, 3–4
Applejack Basting Sauce, 159
Applesauce, 151–52
Armadillo Eggs, A. D.'s, 128–30
Avocado Stuffed with Smoked Turkey, 134

Back Country Turkey, 106
Backwoods Turkey Pilau, 149–50
Bacon, Turkey and, 9
Baked turkey. See Roasted turkey
Baked Turkey Breast, 44–45
Balls, Turkey, 116–17
Barbecued Wild Turkey, 67–68
Basting sauce
  Applejack, 159
  for Larded Turkey, 53
  Lemon Butter, 159–60
Batter-Fried Turkey, 15–16
Bell Peppers, Stuffed, 132–33
Berry(ies)
  Juniper, and Sauce, 160
  Wild Turkey and Wheat Berry
    Porridge, 101–2
Blackened Turkey, 86–87
Boiling. See Stewing
Bon Secour Wild Turkey, 27–28
Bread Dressing, 143–44
Breast
  Baked Turkey, 44–45
  preparation tips, 43–44, 47
  Roast Breast of Wild Turkey, 46–47
  Rock Salt Roast Turkey, 45–46
  on a rotisserie, 47
Broth, for Wild Turkey Tamales, 58
Brunswick Stew, 88–90
Buns, Turkey, 119
Burgers, Turkey, 110–11
Butter Basting Sauce, Lemon, 159–60
Buttermilk Turkey with Gravy, 16–17

Cacciatore, Wild Turkey, 81–82
Caribbean Fried Turkey, 6–7

Caribbean recipes. See Mexican and
  Caribbean recipes
Casserole
  Helen's Latest, 136–38
  Nutty, 133
  Wild Turkey, 130–31
Castillane, Turkey, 56–57
Chestnut Stuffing, Venison Sausage and,
  139–40
Chili, Wild Turkey, 116
Chili Peppers, Stuffed Green, 131–32
Chowder, Peking Turkey, 95–96
Club Sandwich, 122
Coconut Milk, 157–58
Cold Turkey Sandwich, 118–19
Colonial Oyster Sauce, 155–57
Colonial Turkey, 37
Cookers, outdoor. See Smoker-cookers
Corn Bread and Giblet Stuffing, 140–41
Corn Bread for Stuffing or Dressing,
  142–43
Cornmeal Dumplings, 104–5
Country Fried Tom, 4–5
Cracker Stuffing, Easy Oyster and,
  145–46
Cranberry(ies)
  Orange Relish, 151
  Sauce, 150–51
  Turkey Cranberry Sandwich, 121–22
Cranberry Orange Relish, 151
Cranberry Sauce, 150–51
Crockpot dishes
  Crockpot Turkey, 108–9
  Old Tom Crockpot Gumbo, 99–100
Crockpot Turkey, 108–9
Croquettes, Wild Turkey, 10–12
Crusty Baked Wild Turkey, 28–29
Cumberland Sauce, 155

Divan, Murphy Norton, 84–85
Dressing
  Bread, 143–44
  Corn Bread for Stuffing or, 142–43

171

Oyster, 145
Dumplings
    Cornmeal, 104–5
    Turkey with Drop, 103–4
    Wild Turkey and Easy, 105–6

Easy Baked Wild Turkey, 25–26
Easy Dumplings, Wild Turkey and, 105–6
Easy Marinated Turkey, 14–15
Easy Oyster and Cracker Stuffing, 145–46
Easy Sandwich Spread, 122–23
Easy Turkey Loaf, 123
Easy Turkey Nuggets, 8
Easy Turkey Salad, 125
Egg Rolls, Wild Turkey, 13–14
Eggs, A. D.'s Armadillo, 128–30

Fajitas, 55–56
Festive cooking, 20–21
Filé Gumbo, Wild Turkey, 97–99
Fingers
    A. D.'s Fried Turkey, 3–4
    Grilled Turkey, with Garlic Sauce, 71–72
    Skillet Turkey, 83
Fried Pumpkins, 158–59
Fried turkey. *See also* Skillet turkey
    A. D.'s Fried Turkey Fingers, 3–4
    Batter-, 15–16
    Buttermilk Turkey with Gravy, 16–17
    Caribbean, 6–7
    Country Fried Tom, 4–5
    Easy Marinated Turkey, 14–15
    Easy Turkey Nuggets, 8
    Golden Turkey, 12
    Java Turkey, 7–8
    Oven-Fried Turkey Nuggets, 17–18
    preparation tips, 2–3
    reasons for lack of popularity of, 1
    Sessions Whole-, 18–19
    Smother-, 5–6
    Turkey and Bacon, 9
    Vietnamese Stir-Fry, 9–10
    Wild Turkey Croquettes, 10–12
    Wild Turkey Egg Rolls, 13–14

Garlic Sauce, Grilled Turkey Fingers
    with, 71–72
Giblet Gravy, 148–49
Giblet Stuffing, Corn Bread and, 140–41
Golden Turkey, 12
Good Ol' Boy Turkey Kabobs, 74
Goulash, Turkey, 114
Grape Juice, Wild Turkey in, 61–62
Gravy
    Buttermilk Turkey with, 16–17
    Giblet, 148–49
    for Mexican Stuffed Turkey, 55
Green Chili Peppers, Stuffed, 131–32

Grilled turkey
    Barbecued Wild Turkey, 67–68
    Fingers with Garlic Sauce, 71–72
    Good Ol' Boy Turkey Kabobs, 74
    Halves I, 65–66
    Halves II, 66–67
    Island Turkey Kabobs, 75–76
    preparation tips, 63–64
    Sandwiches, 121
    Sesame Turkey, 72–73
    Smoke 'n Grill Turkey, 35
    Strip Steaks, 73
    Tabasco Turkey, 69–70
    Turkey Teriyaki, 68–69
    Turkey with Indonesian Soy Sauce,
        70–71
    Turkey with Piripiri Sauce, 64–65
    Turkish Kabobs, 75
Grilled Turkey Fingers with Garlic
    Sauce, 71–72
Grilled Turkey Halves I, 65–66
Grilled Turkey Halves II, 66–67
Grilled Turkey Sandwiches, 121
Grilled Turkey Strip Steaks, 73
Grills, outdoor. *See* Smoker-cookers
Groundnut Stew, Turkey and, 94–95
Ground turkey
    Italian Turkey Sausage Patties, 113–14
    Old Tom Breakfast Sausage Patties, 113
    preparation tips, 110
    Turkey Balls, 116–17
    Turkey Burgers, 110–11
    Turkey Goulash, 114
    Turkey Patties, 112
    Wild Turkey Chili, 116
    Wild Turkey Sausage Links, 114–15
    Wild Turkey Spaghetti, 111–12
Gumbo
    Old Tom Crockpot, 99–100
    Wild Turkey and Shrimp, 96–97
    Wild Turkey Filé, 97–99

Halves
    Grilled Turkey, I, 65–66
    Grilled Turkey, II, 66–67
Hash, Leftovers, 127
Helen's Favorite, 107–8
Helen's Latest, 136–38
Helen's Rice, 147–48
Honey Mustard Sauce, 154–55

Indonesian Soy Sauce, Turkey with,
    70–71
Island Turkey Kabobs, 75–76
Italian Turkey Sausage Patties, 113–14

Jambalaya, Wild Turkey, 78–79
Java Turkey, 7–8

Juice, Wild Turkey in Grape, 61–62
Juniper Berries and Sauce, 160

Kabobs
    Good Ol' Boy Turkey, 74
    Island Turkey, 75–76
    Turkish, 75
Kumquat Sauce, 152

Larded Turkey, 52–53
Leftovers
    A. D.'s Armadillo Eggs, 128–30
    Avocado Stuffed with Smoked Turkey,
        134
    Easy Turkey Salad, 125
    Helen's Latest, 136–38
    Leftovers Hash, 127
    Nutty Casserole, 133
    Santa Fe Turkey Salad, 134–35
    Stuffed Bell Peppers, 132–33
    Stuffed Green Chili Peppers, 131–32
    Stuffed Tomatoes, 135–36
    Turkey à la King, 130
    Turkey on Toast, 127–28
    Turkey Scrapple, 124–25
    Wild Turkey Casserole, 130–31
    Wild Turkey Salad, 126–27
    Wild Turkey Spread, 136
Leftovers Hash, 127
Lemon Butter Basting Sauce, 159–60
Loaves. *See* Sandwiches and loaves
Louisiana Oyster Stuffing, 144–45

Marengo, Turkey, 80
Marinated Turkey, Easy, 14–15
Mesa, for Wild Turkey Tamales, 58
Metric conversion tables, 169–70
Mexican and Caribbean recipes
    Fajitas, 55–56
    Larded Turkey, 52–53
    Mexican Stuffed Turkey, 53–55
    Molé de Poblano de Guajolote, 49–51
    preparation tips, 48–49
    Turkey Castillane, 56–57
    Turkey Tacos, 60–61
    Wild Turkey in Grape Juice, 61–62
    Wild Turkey Tamales, 58–60
Mexican Stuffed Turkey, 53–55
Middle Eastern Stuffed Turkey, 38–39
Milk, Coconut, 157–58
Missouri Turkey on a Spit, 36–37
Molé de Poblano de Guajolote, 49–51
Murphy Norton Divan, 84–85
Mushroom(s)
    Stuffing, 142
    Turkey and Mushroom Soup, 93–94
Mushroom Stuffing
Mustard Sauce, Honey, 154–55

Noodle(s)
    Soup, 91–93
    Turkey with, 82–83
Noodle Soup, Turkey, 91–93
Nuggets
    Easy Turkey, 8
    Oven-Fried Turkey, 17–18
Nutty Casserole, 133

Old Tom Breakfast Sausage Patties, 113
Old Tom Crockpot Gumbo, 99–100
Open-fire roasting
    Colonial Turkey, 37
    Missouri Turkey on a Spit, 36–37 ·
    preparation tips, 35–36
Orange Relish, Cranberry, 151
Oven-Fried Turkey Nuggets, 17–18
Oyster(s)
    and Cracker Stuffing, Easy, 145–46
    Dressing, 145
    Sauce, Colonial, 155–57
    Stuffing, Louisiana, 144–45
    Turkey with Stewed, 37–38
Oyster Dressing, 145

Paella, Turkey, 90–91
Patties
    Italian Turkey Sausage, 113–14
    Old Tom Breakfast Sausage, 113
    Turkey, 112
Peking Turkey Chowder, 95–96
Pennsylvania Dutch Turkey Stuffing,
        141–42
Peppers, Stuffed
    Bell, 132–33
    Green Chili, 131–32
Pilau, Backwoods Turkey, 149–50
Piripiri Sauce, Turkey with, 64–65
Pit turkey, preparation tips for, 41–43
Plum Sauce
    Sweet Wild, 154
    Wild, 153–54
Pomegranate Syrup, 152–53
Porridge, Wild Turkey and Wheat Berry,
        101–2
Preparation tips, general. *See also under
        individual category, e.g.,* Roasted
        turkey
    ten steps to better wild turkey, 162–68
Pumpkins, Fried, 158–59

Relish, Cranberry Orange, 151
Rice
    Helen's, 147–48
    Smoked Wild Turkey with Wild, 34–35
    Wild, 146–47
Roast Breast of Wild Turkey, 46–47

Roasted (baked) turkey
  Bon Secour Wild Turkey, 27–28
  Breast, 44–45
  Colonial Turkey, 37
  Crusty Baked Wild Turkey, 28–29
  Easy Baked Wild Turkey, 25–26
  Missouri Turkey on a Spit, 36–37
  open-fire roasting, 35–37
  preparation tips, 23–25, 35–36
  Roast Breast of Wild Turkey, 46–47
  Rock Salt Roast Turkey Breast, 45–46
  Steve Juhan's Wild Turkey, 29–30
  Stuffed Turkey, 26–27
Rock Salt Roast Turkey Breast, 45–46
Rotisserie, breast on a, 47

Salad
  Easy Turkey, 125
  Santa Fe Turkey, 134–35
  Wild Turkey, 126–27
Salsa, 157
Sandwiches and loaves
  Club Sandwich, 122
  Cold Turkey Sandwich, 118–19
  Easy Sandwich Spread, 122–23
  Easy Turkey Loaf, 123
  Grilled Turkey Sandwiches, 121
  preparation tips, 118
  Sloppy Joes with Turkey, 120
  Turkey Buns, 119
  Turkey Cranberry Sandwich, 121–22
Santa Fe Turkey Salad, 134–35
Sauce(s)
  Apple-, 151–52
  Applejack Basting, 159
  for Barbecued Wild Turkey, 68
  Basting, for Larded Turkey, 53
  Coconut Milk, 157–58
  Colonial Oyster, 155–57
  Cranberry, 150–51
  Cumberland, 155
  Garlic, Grilled Turkey Fingers with,
     71–72
  Honey Mustard, 154–55
  Indonesian Soy, Turkey with, 70–71
  Juniper Berries and, 160
  Kumquat, 152
  Lemon Butter Basting, 159–60
  Piquante, Turkey, 83–84
  Piripiri, Turkey with, 64–65
  Salsa, 157
  Sweet Wild Plum, 154
  Wild Plum, 153–54
Sausage
  Links, Wild Turkey, 114–15
  Patties, Italian Turkey, 113–14
  Patties, Old Tom Breakfast, 113
  Venison, and Chestnut Stuffing, 139–40

Scrapple, Turkey, 124–25
Sesame Turkey, 72–73
Sessions Whole-Fried Turkey, 18–19
Shrimp Gumbo, Wild Turkey and, 96–97
Skillet turkey. *See also* Fried turkey
  Blackened Turkey, 86–87
  Murphy Norton Divan, 84–85
  preparation tips, 77
  Skillet Stir-Fry, 79–80
  Skillet Turkey Fingers, 83
  Turkey Marengo, 80
  Turkey Sauce Piquante, 83–84
  Wild Turkey and Swamp Cabbage,
     85–86
  Wild Turkey Cacciatore, 81–82
  Wild Turkey Jambalaya, 78–79
Skillet Stir-Fry, 79–80
Skillet Turkey Fingers, 83
Sloppy Joes with Turkey, 120
Smoked turkey
  Avocado Stuffed with, 134
  preparation tips, 33
  Smoked Wild Turkey with Wild Rice, 34
  Smoke 'n' Grill Turkey, 35
  smoker-cookers for, 24–25, 30–33
Smoked Wild Turkey with Wild Rice, 34
Smoke 'n' Grill Turkey, 35
Smoker-cookers, 24–25
  barrel and tank grills, 32
  box grills, 32
  jackleg smokers, 33
  pyramid system, 32
  round and kettle grills, 32
  silo units, 30–32
  stand-up smokers, 32–33
Smother-Fried Turkey, 5–6
Soused Tom Turkey, 40–41
Soup
  Helen's Favorite, 107–8
  Peking Turkey Chowder, 95–96
  Turkey and Mushroom, 93–94
  Turkey Noodle, 91–93
Soy Sauce, Turkey with Indonesian, 70–71
Spaghetti, Wild Turkey, 111–12
Spit, Missouri Turkey on a, 36–37
Spread
  Easy Sandwich, 122–23
  Wild Turkey, 136
Steaks, Grilled Turkey Strip, 73
Steve Juhan's Wild Turkey Roast, 29–30
Stew
  Back Country Turkey, 106
  Brunswick, 88–90
  Cornmeal Dumplings, 104–5
  Crockpot Turkey, 108–9
  Helen's Favorite, 107–8
  Old Tom Crockpot Gumbo, 99–100
  preparation tips, 88

Stewed Wild Turkey, 107
Turkey and Groundnut, 94–95
Turkey and Walnut, 102
Turkey Paella, 90–91
Turkey with Drop Dumplings, 103–4
Wild Turkey, 107
Wild Turkey and Easy Dumplings, 105–6
Wild Turkey and Shrimp Gumbo, 96–97
Wild Turkey and Wheat Berry Porridge, 101–2
Wild Turkey Filé Gumbo, 97–99
Stewing (boiling)
Middle Eastern Stuffed Turkey, 38–40
preparation tips, 37
Soused Tom Turkey, 40–41
Turkey with Stewed Oysters, 37–38
Stir-Fry
Skillet, 79–80
Vietnamese, 9–10
Stock, Turkey, 160–61
Stuffed Bell Peppers, 132–33
Stuffed Green Chili Peppers, 131–32
Stuffed Tomatoes, 135–36
Stuffed turkey
Mexican, 53–55
Middle Eastern, 38–39
Stuffing
Corn Bread and Giblet, 140–41
Corn Bread for Dressing or, 142–43
Easy Oyster and Cracker, 145–46
Louisiana Oyster, 144–45
for Mexican Stuffed Turkey, 54
Pennsylvania Dutch Turkey, 141–42
Mushroom, 142
Venison Sausage and Chestnut, 139–40
Swamp Cabbage, Wild Turkey and, 85–86
Sweet Wild Plum Sauce, 154
Syrup, Pomegranate, 152–53

Tabasco Turkey, 69–70
Tacos, Turkey, 60–61
Tamales, Wild Turkey, 58–60
Temperature
crucial, 21–22, 24
thermometer for, 22–24
Teriyaki, Turkey, 68–69
Thermometer, meat, 22–23
Toast, Turkey on, 127–28
Tom turkey
Country Fried, 4–5
Old Tom Breakfast Sausage Patties, 113
Old Tom Crockpot Gumbo, 99–100
Soused, 40–41
Tomatoes, Stuffed, 135–36
Trussing, 23
Turkey à la King, 130

Turkey and Bacon, 9
Turkey and Groundnut Stew, 94–95
Turkey and Mushroom Soup, 93–94
Turkey and Walnut Stew, 102
Turkey Balls, 116–17
Turkey Buns, 119
Turkey Burgers, 110–11
Turkey Castillane, 56–57
Turkey Cranberry Sandwich, 121–22
Turkey Goulash, 114
Turkey Marengo, 80
Turkey Noodle Soup, 91–93
Turkey on Toast, 127–28
Turkey Paella, 90–91
Turkey Patties, 112
Turkey Sauce Piquante, 83–84
Turkey Scrapple, 124–25
Turkey Stock, 160–61
Turkey Tacos, 60–61
Turkey Teriyaki, 68–69
Turkey with Drop Dumplings, 103–4
Turkey with Indonesian Soy Sauce, 70–71
Turkey with Noodles, 82–83
Turkey with Piripiri Sauce, 64–65
Turkey with Stewed Oysters, 37–38
Turkish Kabobs, 75

Venison Sausage and Chestnut Stuffing, 139–40
Vietnamese Stir-Fry, 9–10

Walnut Stew, Turkey and, 102
Wheat Berry Porridge, Wild Turkey and, 101–2
Whole-Fried Turkey, Sessions, 18–19
Wild Plum Sauce, 153–54
Sweet, 154
Wild Rice, 146–47
Wild Rice, Smoked Wild Turkey with, 34
Wild Turkey and Easy Dumplings, 105–6
Wild Turkey and Shrimp Gumbo, 96–97
Wild Turkey and Swamp Cabbage, 85–86
Wild Turkey and Wheat Berry Porridge, 101–2
Wild Turkey Cacciatore, 81–82
Wild Turkey Casserole, 130–31
Wild Turkey Chili, 116
Wild Turkey Croquettes, 10–12
Wild Turkey Egg Rolls, 13–14
Wild Turkey Filé Gumbo, 97–99
Wild Turkey in Grape Juice, 61–62
Wild Turkey Jambalaya, 78–79
Wild Turkey Salad, 126–27
Wild Turkey Sausage Links, 114–15
Wild Turkey Spaghetti, 111–12
Wild Turkey Spread, 136
Wild Turkey Tamales, 58–60